Karl Marx

Karl Marx

Colin Gumbrell

Series Editors
Michael and Mollie Hardwick

Evergreen Lives

©1983 Evergreen Lives
All rights reserved
No part of this publication may be reproduced,
stored in a retrieval system, or transmitted in
any form or by any means, electronic, mechanical,
photocopying, recording or otherwise, without the
prior written permission of the publishers.

ISBN 0 7127 0006 4

Series Editors
Michael and Mollie Hardwick

Design by Roy Lee

Production by Bob Towell

Colour Separations
by
D.S. Colour International Limited, London
Photo-typesetting
by
Sayers Clark Limited, Croydon, Surrey

Printed and bound in Spain by
TONSA, San Sebastian

Contents

Select Bibliography	9
Chronology	10
Introduction	13
A Dark Form from Trier	21
Paris - the Place to Be	31
The Coming of Communism	39
Tide of Revolution	49
'Hellish Muck'	57
Poverty, Illness - and 'Capital'	67
A 'Powerful Machine'	79
The Fire Goes Out	87
Illustrated Life	97
Acknowledgements	128

Select Bibliography

I. BERLIN - *Karl Marx. His life and Environment.* (London 1970)

WERNER BLUMENBERG - *Karl Marx* (London 1972)

YVONNE KAPP - *Eleanor Marx*, 2 Vols (London 1972 and 1976)

A. KETTLE - *Karl Marx, Founder of Modern Communism* (London 1963)

KARL MARX and FRIEDRICH ENGELS - *Selected Correspondence* (London 1965)

F. MEHRING - *Karl Marx, the Story of His Life* (London 1951)

I. FETSCHER - *Marx and Marxism* (New York 1971)

E. FISCHER - *Marx in his Own Words* (London 1971)

PETER SINGER - *Marx* (Oxford 1980)

Chronology

1814 Jenny von Westphalen born.

1818 Karl Marx born 5 May in Trier, in the South Rhineland of Germany.

1820 Friedrich Engels born.

1835 Marx enters Bonn University as law student in October.

1836 Enters Berlin University, October. Engaged to Jenny von Westphalen.

1838 Death of Marx's father, Heinrich.

1841 Gains degree in philosophy from Jena University.

1842 His first published article appears in *Rhenish Gazette* in March. He becomes its editor in October.

1843 *Rhenish Gazette* closes in March. Karl and Jenny marry, 19 June, and move to Paris in October. He edits the *Franco-German Annals*.

1844 First daughter Jenny born 1 May. Marx and Engels meet in September and begin a lifelong friendship.

1845 Marx expelled from France in January. Moves to Brussels. Visits England with Engels July/August. They collaborate on *The German Ideology*. Jenny's mother's maid Helene Demuth ('Lenchen') joins the Marx household. Birth of Laura in September.

1846 First son Edgar born in December.

1847 First congress of the Communist League in London in June. Marx in London for second congress in December.

1848 The *Communist Manifesto* published by Marx in February. Expelled from Belgium in March. Family move to Paris then Cologne where Marx founds the *New Rhenish Gazette*.

1849 Marx tried for subversion in Cologne but acquitted. The *New Rhenish Gazette* ceases publication with its 'Red Number' in May. Expelled from Prussia, Marx goes to England, soon joined by his family. They live at 4 Anderson Street, Chelsea, where second son Henry ('Guido') is born.

1850 Evicted from Anderson Street in March and move to 28 Dean Street, Soho. 'Guido' dies in September.

1851 Births of Franziska Marx and Frederick Demuth, Marx's son by 'Lenchen'. A period of dire poverty and Communist League squabbles.

1852 Death of Franziska. Marx begins writing regularly for *New York Daily Tribune*. Engels begins supporting him financially.

1855 Eleanor Marx born in January. Edgar dies in April.

1856 The family moves to 9 Grafton Terrace, Kentish Town, in September.

1859 Marx's *Critique of Political Economy* published.

1861 Marx visits Holland and Germany.

1863 Marx's mother dies in November, her legacy relieving the family's poverty.

1864 Move to 1 Maitland Park Road, Haverstock Hill. International Working Men's Association founded, 28 September.

1866 First congress of The International in Geneva.

1867 First volume of *Capital* published, 14 September.

1871 Formation of Paris Commune in March and collapse in May.

1875 Family move to 41 Maitland Park Road.

1881 Marx's wife Jenny dies, 2 December.

1883 Karl Marx dies, 14 March.

Introduction

KARL MARX'S TOMB in Highgate Cemetery, North London, a huge block surmounted by a monster bust, draws people from all over the world. All day and every day they come, enquiring in varied accents for its whereabouts; some, perhaps, surprised to find it in a Christian graveyard, since Marx, born a Jew, renounced the Christianity his father had adopted. In fact, the section in which he was buried in 1883 was at that time undenominational.

By night, from time to time, other visitors come, armed with pots of red paint. For, offsetting the many who worship Marx and subscribe to his theories, there are many others who deplore his existence and its consequences. Yet do even the worshippers know much of him, or what he really thought and said? George Bernard Shaw wrote in 1911:

> Twenty-five years ago it was fashionable in English socialist circles to say that one had read Karl Marx and Friedrich Engels, and I read the famous first volume of *Das Kapitel* too, only to discover that nobody else had, and that it contained not a word about what socialism was. But I consider that Marx was not really an author - either German or any other nationality. He was an anti-bourgeois and his battle cry was, 'Anti-bourgeois of all countries, unite to

Karl Marx

> fight', which they still do every three years. The world is greatly indebted to Marx for his description of the selfishness and stupidity of that respected middle class so worshipped in Germany and England, and *Das Kapital* is one of those books that changes people if they can be persuaded to read it. However, it is the work of a man who was not a member of normal German or English society and who wrote about capitalists and workers like a class-war correspondent.

It is probably true to say, even today, that *Capital* is one of the most mentioned and least read books in the world.

Marx the man is almost as unknown. If he has an image at all, it is that of the fiercely-bearded ogre on the tomb. This book sets out to show him as a human being, and the portrait is a surprising one, from the initial discovery that he, so closely identified with late nineteenth-century socialism, was born in 1818, two years before the Prince Regent became King George the Fourth; like Charles Dickens, born six years earlier, he was in English terms not a Victorian, but a Georgian.

He was a descendant of many generations of rabbis, though he later preferred to forget it, and to profess contempt for Jews and Judaism. He did not belong to the class to which he proclaimed lifelong loyalty, the workers; his background was solidly bourgeois, his father a lawyer, later a magistrate. The family life of the Marxes was happy, cosy, full of characteristically German warmth and sentimentality. Karl grew up into a normal student of his time, with the usual record of drinking and duelling, and a passion for writing romantic poetry, full of the sort of wild melancholy that emanates from the lyrics of Heine and the songs of Schubert.

Romantic not only on paper, he fell violently in love with the beautiful Jenny von Westphalen, the descendant of Scottish aristocrats. Her lovely gentle face looks out serenely from a girlhood portrait; in a photograph taken towards the end of her life it has become haggard, soured, disappointed.

Introduction

'The most beautiful girl in Trier', 'the Queen of the ball', had been sadly changed by many years with a husband she loved to the end.

For Marx, who wanted to change for the better the lives of countless millions, was, like so many idealists, completely incapable of managing his own. Jenny and her children were dragged down with him into abject poverty, misery and squalor. Evicted from lodgings, too poor to buy a cradle for a baby daughter whose next requirement was a coffin, living in a strange country - England - in conditions as bad as any, surely, that Marx and Engels had seen in their investigation of the English poor, the story of their sufferings is a tragic one. Marx, born into the bourgeoisie, naturally wished to support his family comfortably, and they achieved something like it in the last years at Hampstead. But by then it was too late for most of them; tuberculosis and cancer had taken hold, and the seeds of tragedy been sown. His daughter Eleanor, after a long and fraught association with Dr Edward Aveling, committed suicide in 1898, her sister Laura in 1911. Their eldest sister Jenny had died aged only thirty-nine in the same year as her father. But for the financial support Marx received from the wealthy Engels, first by borrowing and then by a settled allowance, the family might well have ended up in the workhouse. And - a curious thought - but for Engels's capital there might have been no Marxism.

Yet Jenny, for all her suffering, loved Karl constantly and deeply, and Eleanor was devoted to him, his closest companion after her mother's death, writing of him as 'the kindest and gentlest of men...he could hate so fiercely only because he could love so profoundly.' In other relationships he was inadequate, too preoccupied with theory to concern himself with individuals. Perhaps he was not even interested in them. The English character, with its unique combination of individuality and eccentricity, must have been a mystery to him, and he had no comprehension of the men who made up the masses he fought for. Shaw analysed it neatly: *Capital*, he said 'was addressed to the working classes; but the working man respects the bourgeoisie, and wants to be a bourgeois. It was the revolting sons of the bourgeoisie itself...who painted the flag red.'

Marx's imperfections of character, which stood between him and any kind of happiness or normality, were the price paid for being a little larger than life. Born into a period when misery and exploitation were the fate of the industrial working classes, the age of rick-burning and machine-smashing, he was a powerful and timely friend to those who had no friends, a man of extraordinary vision and political insight. He wrote 'In the social production of their means of existence men enter into definite and unavoidable relations which are independent of their will. These productive relationships correspond to the particular stage in the development of their material forces.' His power of prophecy was weak, for he foretold that socialism would replace capitalism in Europe by means of revolution, and that the one country in which this would not happen was Russia. His doctrine was that 'man is the highest being for man; i.e. the categorical imperative to overthrow all conditions in which man is a humiliated, enslaved, despised and rejected being'.

History has proved him wrong about almost everything. His insistence on the all-importance of class struggle in the history of society is not, by any standards, true. His advocacy of revolution as the inevitable instrument of social change was mistaken; changes have taken place by means of laws and reforms, in a perfectly peaceful way. His view of the 'wicked capitalist', owning factories and using his wealth and power to exploit the innocent worker, is as out of date as the Wicked Landlord of melodrama evicting the innocent heroine and her old father; it was rapidly becoming out of date at the time he published it. His picture of society was vastly over-simplified, and the terms used in *Capital* now read like descriptions of some fabulous fictional country. Poverty, oppression, enslavement, degeneration, exploitation;

Introduction

the anger of the working class; the death knell of capitalist private property: all these are empty phrases, in the light of what has actually happened since he coined them.

He expected, in 1848, a bourgeois revolution in Germany. It did not happen. He expected a unity among the members of the proletariat which was impossible, by reason of the differences which have always existed between one person and another, something he could not comprehend because he failed to understand people. His political view was so limited that he failed to take into account the circumstances which were leading towards the total war of 1914, which would swallow up capitalist and worker alike.

His ethical values seem to have been non-existent, since he took no heed of existing cultures and their certain destruction in the revolutions he wanted: for example, the demise of the religious, artistic and traditional elements which characterised the Czech and Polish peoples before the Communist takeover.

There is, in fact, no such thing as Marxism pure and simple, nor would it be easy for one who professed it to define it precisely. His doctrines have become confused with those of Engels, Lenin, Stalin, and even Mao Tse-tung. Among the variations are Revisionism, Titoism, Khruschevism and Castroism. Few terms as used as loosely as 'Marxism', and it would be surprising to find that many who profess it have studied and analysed it at all deeply.

Comparision is inevitable between Marx, the political dreamer and idealist, and another Utopian without roots in reality, William Morris, nineteenth-century Pre-Raphaelite and socialist. The vast gulf between them was that Morris was a lover of art and beauty, who saw politics as a means to the general happiness and oneness of mankind.

> Forsooth, brothers, fellowship is heaven, and lack of fellowship is hell: fellowship is life, and lack of fellowship is death: and the deeds that you do upon the earth, it is for fellowship's sake that ye do them.

Karl Marx

Morris longed for an olde England which had never existed except in his imagination. In his *News from Nowhere* he visualised a purer England, in the main pastoral, all commerce and machinery done away with, laws and currency gone, the exchange of handicrafts the only commerce left. Dirty late-Victorian Hammersmith, where his Kelmscott House was, was envisaged as a lovely, clean Thames-side stretch, where everything is made by hand and the whirr of the spinning-wheel has superseded the clatter of machinery. Details of how it is all supposed to have come about are vague, though in the chapter 'How the Change Came' there are hints which have been taken up by Marxists as having been inspired by *Capital*. But the character Old Hammond says, 'We are very well off as to politics - because we have none.' Morris himself said, 'I think as in a vision, of a decent community as a refuge from our squabbles and corrupt society.' He wrote of himself:

> Dreamer of dreams, born out of my due time,
> Why should I strive to set the crooked straight?

His notion of revolution, in *The Dream of John Ball*, is something bloodless and thoroughly therapeutic. He at least knew that he was a dreamer, a theorist; Marx, the Prussian without aesthetic or moral sensibility, did not even pause to think about it. And so their works remain, both quoted as blueprints for a communist state, and Marx's News from Nowhere is every bit as unrealistic as Morris's, and a great deal less attractive.

An English national newspaper which features a cartoon strip based on topical comments postulated the return to life in the 1980s of a Marx tired of the Highgate clay. Seething with revolutionary zeal he marched about England, pausing frequently to rub his eyes and doubt their evidence: the humiliated, enslaved, despised, rejected workers enjoying colour television, washing machines, cars, holidays on the Costa del Chips? The oppressed sons of toil bringing the nation to a standstill, as they struck for another addition to their wages? The accents of the proletariat on the lips of the aristocracy, fearful of being thought superior or different?

So the spectral Marx, beard wilting, crept back to his coffin and his niche in history. Of that, at least, nobody would ever dispossess him.

Michael and Mollie Hardwick

A Dark Form from Trier

1818 – 1843

AT BRÜCKERGASSE 664 (now Brückenstrasse 10 and a museum to his memory), in the city of Trier in the south Rhineland, Karl Marx was born on 5 May 1818.

His birthplace is a city steeped in history. As Augusta Treverorum it was a provincial capital of the Roman Empire, while in the Middle Ages it became the seat of a powerful archdiocese. But by the end of the eighteenth century a new age, heralded by the French Revolution, had dawned in Europe. Its influence was felt in Trier in 1794, when the Rhineland was annexed by France.

For the next twenty years, most of Trier's population of about 15,000 enjoyed a measure of constitutional liberty largely unknown in the rest of Germany. Even the oppressed Jewish community was granted nominal equality; but the Jews' freedom of movement and licence to trade were still severely restricted, so it was with a degree of optimism that they greeted the prospect of new masters when, at the Congress of Vienna in 1814, the Rhineland was awarded to Prussia. They soon found Prussian rule to be even worse. It became impossible for a Jew to hold a position in the service of the state without a royal dispensation, and in 1818 a decree was issued retaining the harsher of the Napoleonic laws indefinitely.

One of the Jews of Trier whose security was threatened was a lawyer named Hirschel Marx. He and his wife Henrietta were of the purest Jewish blood, both descended from long lines of rabbinical families. Hirschel was hardly a staunch upholder of this tradition: he had broken early with his family and felt no affinity with other Jews. His chief concern was his profession, which he had to maintain to preserve his family from poverty. Under Prussian rule he could keep his job only by changing his religion, which he did without compunction. He did not join the vast Catholic majority of Trier's population, but chose to become a Protestant, so attaching himself to a minority of only about two hundred. He was baptised some time before August 1817 and changed his name to Heinrich. Thus the Marx family, though comfortably middle-class, was to some extent alienated both from its ancestors and its environment.

The third child born into this family, after a son who died in 1819 aged four, and a daughter, Sophie, born in 1816, was named Karl Heinrich.

In childhood, Karl was strongly attached to his elder sister Sophie; but in later life, after she had married and moved to Maastricht in Holland, he hardly kept in touch with her. Of six more children born to the Marxes, only two sisters survived past the age of forty.

As a boy, Karl was a boisterous and domineering brother, to judge from a few reminiscences of these sisters, recounted when they were grown old to his daughter Eleanor. He would drive the girls along as if they were horses at full gallop, and make them eat dirty dough cakes that he had made with grubby hands. Afterwards, he rewarded them for putting up with this treatment by telling them wonderful stories.

Up to 1830 he was probably educated at home. The influence of his mother, about whom little is known, is a matter for conjecture. It seems likely that she retained something of her Jewish identity, as she was not baptised until 1825, a year after Karl's baptism. His father is a figure much clearer to posterity. He was closely involved in the Rhineland liberal movement, yet, paradoxically, there

A Dark Form from Trier

was also a proud vein of Prussian patriotism in him. His Christianity took the form of a lukewarm but sincere deism, as epitomised in a letter to his student son: 'There are moments in life when even the man who denies God is compelled against his will to pray to the Almighty.'

Almost as important a mentor to Karl as his father was Baron Ludwig von Westphalen. Since he worked in the same legal service in Trier as Heinrich Marx, and was also a Protestant, it was natural for him and Heinrich to become friends, and their families, who were anyway close neighbours, gravitated towards each other. The Baron, an intelligent, well-read man, took Karl under his wing. Besides introducing him to the works of Homer and Shakespeare, he instilled in him a love of romantic poetry. Meanwhile, the Baron's daughter, Jenny, four years older than Karl, had become a close friend of Sophie Marx, and Karl saw her often.

From 1830 to 1835 he attended the secondary school in Trier, where he received a solidly humanist education. Karl was only a moderate pupil, whose weakest subject, oddly enough, was history. His religion was satisfactory; in an essay for his Abitur, the school-leaving examination, on 'the reason, nature, necessity and effects of the union of believers with Christ', he showed a sound ability of reason, flawed by an over-pious style and a vague, deistic notion of God, clearly inherited from his father. His German composition for the Abitur was original; titled 'Reflections of a Young Man on the Choice of Career', its theme was the need for the man setting out in life to be sure to take the chance to work for the good of humanity. Karl proclaimed in it that 'History calls those the greatest men who ennoble themselves by working for the universal...When we have chosen the vocation in which we can contribute most to humanity, burdens cannot bend us because they are only sacrifices for all. Then...our happiness belongs to millions, our deeds live on quietly but eternally effective, and glowing tears of noble men will fall on our ashes.'

In October 1835 he left for university in Bonn. Having registered in the Law Faculty he studied keenly during the first term. Following an illness caused by overworking he reduced the number of his courses from six to four, and took to socialising and drinking, running up large debts which his father was obliged to pay. His increasingly reckless way of life came to a head when, in August 1836, he fought a duel and was wounded over the left eye. His other main preoccupation was the writing of poems, some of which he sent home for approval on the rare occasions he wrote to his family. His father found them unfathomable and soon decided that Karl should move from the heady, romantic atmosphere of Bonn to the more sedate Berlin University.

In the summer vacation of 1836, though, heady romance was uppermost in Karl's mind. As he had promised her before going to Bonn, he became engaged to Jenny von Westphalen. She was a beautiful, auburn-haired, green-eyed girl, who had many suitors in Trier but none as insistent and persuasive as Karl, who later called himself 'a really furious Roland'. For all the intimacy of their families, Karl and Jenny preferred their engagement to be at first a secret, known only to his parents and Sophie, as they feared that Jenny's family would disapprove: she belonged to a higher social class than Karl, besides being so much older. Their fears were well founded. Apart from Jenny's father, who readily gave his consent to the match when he was told about it in March 1837, and her mother, the rest of her 'pietistaristocratic relations', as Marx later termed them, were vehemently opposed, presaging 'years of unnecessary and exhausting conflicts' between them and the young lovers.

Leaving his family to cope with the secret, Karl went off in October 1836 to Berlin, described by a contemporary as a workhouse by comparison with the 'Bacchanalian' character of other universities. He stayed there for the next four and a half years.

Before long he was busily composing lyric poems, all dedicated, and dispatched in three collections, to Jenny. According to Sophie she

A Dark Form from Trier

wept 'tears of delight and pain' over these expressions of Karl's love. Though Jenny kept these early works all her life none of them survive. Only fragments of a few other poems written by Marx in early 1837 remain. They express the conflict in the ego of the creative writer, at once loftily isolated from the mass of humanity and yet yearning to find others of kindred spirit. Gone for now was the idealistic desire to serve mankind from his Abitur essay. But these poems were symptoms of a passing phase of youth, and the adult Marx was soon to emerge from the chrysalis. He had decided to 'struggle with philosophy'; and the philosophy rampant in Berlin was Hegelianism.

G.W.F. Hegel had been professor of philosophy at Berlin from 1818 to his death in 1831. His 'Absolute Idealism', developing the ideas of Kant, Fichte and Schelling, is notoriously difficult to comprehend; it is also crucial to an understanding of Marx's thought. There follows a much-simplified summary of its essence.

In Kant's system, there was an inherent dualism: the opposition of spirit to nature, of master to slave, and so on, which was irreconcilable. It was Hegel's aim to unify this dualism. All difference, he argued, presupposed a unity, i.e. a definite thing or thought could not be separated from its opposite: the slave could not exist without the master, and vice versa. Hegel's idea was that this unity would be eventually realised in the equalising of all opposites, by means of the dialectic (logical progression) of thesis - antithesis - synthesis, which provided his theory of the evolving process of history.

It is perhaps best illustrated by an example from the *Phenomenology of Mind*, the work Marx was to describe as 'the true birthplace and secret' of his own philosophy. Imagine the relationship of master and slave. Superficially, it seems the master is all and the slave nothing; but it is the slave who does the work and so changes the natural world. So, in asserting his consciousness over the world, the slave develops his own self-consciousness, while the idle master is dependent on him. In the end, the mind of the slave is liberated, and he and the master are no longer opposed. The situation has proceeded from the thesis of master dominating slave, through the antithesis of slave dominating master, to the final synthesis of their equality.

All depends on the concept of *Weltgeist* - Universal Mind. This, according to Hegel, was total, all-embracing spirit, of which each human mind was but a part. Moreover, each human mind was unaware of the existence of Mind, and so considered other human minds alien, hostile, whereas they were all part of the same thing. So all oppositions were but illusions fostered by human minds, and would be obliterated as soon as Mind was recognized. Eventually, by way of the dialectic, complete freedom would be achieved, as opposites were synthesized into equality.

It was during a period of convalescence after a severe illness that Marx immersed himself in Hegel's writings. He emerged converted to Hegelianism, and, spreading his new-found wings, joined the Berlin Doctors' Club, the nerve-centre of the Young Hegelian movement.

The Young Hegelians were by no means uncritical of their master. For Hegel, although religion was a form of alienation in that it separated humble man from exalted God, it nonetheless represented the efforts of human minds to return to Mind, and so was an acceptable form of activity. But the Young Hegelians, who interpreted Hegel's idea of Mind freeing itself from alienation to mean human consciousness freeing itself from illusions to achieve self-knowledge, saw religion as the biggest illusion of all. In the Doctors' Club, Marx fell under the influence of Bruno Bauer, a subversive lecturer in theology who convinced him of the Young Hegelian beliefs.

From the following description of Marx in a satirical poem by Edgar Bauer, Bruno's brother, we can see that the student Karl was not a shy young man:

> But who advances here full of impetuosity?
> It is a dark form from Trier, an unleashed monster,

A Dark Form from Trier

> With self-assured step he hammers the ground with his heels
> And raises his arms in full fury to heaven
> As though he wished to seize the celestial vault and lower it to earth.
> In rage he continually deals with redoubtable fist,
> As if a thousand devils were gripping his hair.

The Bohemian behaviour of the 'Dark Form from Trier' was estranging him from his father. Heinrich expressed his dismay succinctly in a distraught letter to his son: 'Degeneration in a learned dressing-gown with uncombed hair has replaced degeneration with a beer glass.'

Karl was never truly reconciled with his father, but he did have a deep affection for him, and it was a bitter blow when Heinrich Marx died in May 1838. The blow was financial as well as emotional; the family's income was suddenly much reduced, and it became a matter of urgency for Karl to find a career. He embarked on a doctoral thesis that would enable him to be a lecturer in philosophy, preferably at Bonn, where Bruno Bauer had been sent. He spent two years working on this, submitting it to the University of Jena in April 1841. It constituted a discussion of contrasts between the philosophies of Democritus and Epicurus, in which Marx saw parallels with the philosophies of his own time. The most striking passage pronounced the supremacy of philosophy over religion, taking the proclamation of Prometheus - 'In a word - I hate all gods' - as philosophy's 'slogan against all gods of heaven and earth who do not recognize man's self-consciousness as the highest divinity.'

It was known to be easy to obtain a doctorate at Jena, and there was no delay in the granting of Marx's degree, which he received on 15 April. He was now Dr Marx; but the academic career he sought was not to be.

After spending six weeks in Trier, he moved to Bonn, hoping to join forces with Bauer. Bauer was in trouble with the authorities for his outspoken atheism, and by mid-1842 had been dismissed from his post.

Several projects which the young men had planned together had come to nothing when, in December 1841, Marx was recalled to Trier to be with Baron von Westphalen, who was seriously ill. Marx stayed to comfort his old mentor, to whom he had dedicated his thesis, until the latter died on 3 March 1842. When he returned to Bonn, Bauer was out of work, and Marx's hopes of a university career evaporated.

A new door opened straight away. While in Trier he had written an article exposing the hypocrisy of the censorship regulations recently issued by the new King Friedrich Wilhelm IV, and sent it to Arnold Ruge, editor of a Young Hegelian periodical. Not surprisingly, the article was suppressed by the censors and did not appear until February 1843 in a collection of similarly banned pieces published in Switzerland. The chief consequence was that Marx had established contact with Ruge, who encouraged him to press on with journalism.

In April 1842, Marx moved to Cologne, seeking a more congenial atmosphere than he found in Bonn among the orthodox professors. What he found in Cologne is summed up in a letter to him from the adoring Jenny: 'My dark little savage, how glad I am that you are happy, that my letter exhilarated you, that you long for me, that you live in well-prepared rooms, that you have drunk champagne in Cologne, that there are Hegel clubs there, that you have dreamed and, in short, that you are my darling, my own dark little savage.' But his stay was short-lived, for although he enjoyed it in small doses he no longer relished the high life as much as he had in student days. What he really wanted was time for serious philosophy, so he went back to Bonn and the company of Bauer. But the latter soon left for Berlin, and their ways parted for ever.

Marx continued to visit Cologne. Despite Jenny's advice against participation in practical politics he became involved in the city's liberal opposition movement, and especially its focal point, the 'Cologne Circle'. His closest friend there was Georg Jung, who said that Marx, 'although a devil of a revolutionary', was 'one of the most penetrating minds I know'. Another prominent member was Moses Hess, one of the first German communists, who introduced Marx to a friend thus: 'Prepare to meet the greatest - perhaps the only genuine - philosopher now alive... Imagine Rousseau, Voltaire, Holbach, Lessing, Heine and Hegel fused into one person - I say fused not juxtaposed - and you have Dr Marx.'

The Circle was running a newspaper, the *Rhenish Gazette (Rheinische Zeitung)*, financed by a company of wealthy liberals, to propagate its views, supporting the equality of all citizens and the political and economic unification of Germany. Marx's first published article appeared in it in March 1842. It was a defence of the freedom of the Press, and was warmly acclaimed by his friends.

In the summer of 1842, after a violent quarrel while he was staying in Trier because of a death in the family, his mother withdrew all financial aid. They had never been close, and the rift between them was more or less permanent, though she was to be generous enough to him in future times of need. For now, he was on his own, and journalism seemed his best hope of making a living. When it became clear that Rutenberg, the incompetent editor of the *Rhenish Gazette*, was ripe for replacement, Marx seized his opportunity by writing a letter to the holding company, outlining the way he would run the paper. He opposed 'striking an attitude against the present pillars of the state' which 'could only result in a tightening of the censorship and even in the suppression of the paper.' This was an amazingly moderate stance for Marx, and he got what he wanted when, on 15 October 1842, he was made editor-in-chief. Now, of necessity, he moved back to Cologne.

His first editorial task was to rebuff an accusation that his paper was sympathetic to communism, which he flatly denied, while admitting that communistic ideas, like all ideas, should be taken seriously, as ideas were more powerful than action in influencing people.

Karl Marx

Marx may not yet have been a communist, but he was certainly giving his ear to the socialist ideas being spread through Germany by a number of young intellectuals. Among them was Moses Hess, who founded a group which was in effect the *Rhenish Gazette's* editorial committee, and held monthly seminars in the paper's offices. Through these, Marx's interest in social questions was stimulated and he was moved to make a study of socio-economic conditions in the Rhineland. This resulted in an article condemning new laws that forbade the gathering of dead wood from forests, which had been declared theft. He followed this with a well-researched and indignant couple of articles, published in January 1843, on the poverty of the Mosel wine-farmers; and it was in the writing of these articles, as Engels said later, that Marx was led 'from pure politics to economic relationships and so to socialism'.

Marx had long since abandoned his moderate tone, growing in outspoken confidence as the paper's circulation more than doubled. The *Rhenish Gazette* was now blatantly criticizing the Prussian régime, which was more than the Prussian régime would stand. Other liberal papers had already been banned, and on 21 January 1843 the King's Council of Ministers resolved to suppress the *Rhenish Gazette*. On 17 March Marx resigned and his paper expired. It caused him little sorrow; he wrote to Ruge, 'the Government have given me back my liberty.' He was finding the political climate in Germany unbearably oppressive and was determined to leave his homeland. The question was where to go?

Paris — the Place to Be

1843 – 1845

JENNY HAD WAITED PATIENTLY for him since their engagement seven years ago. To marry needed money, and now he was unemployed. Fortunately, Arnold Ruge was involved in a project to start up a new review outside Germany. Marx jumped at the invitation to be his co-editor, assured of a decent salary now that a publisher willing to share expenses with Ruge had been found.

At last he could marry his childhood sweetheart. He no longer wrote poetry for her, but his feelings were as intense as ever. Jenny was living with her mother in Kreuznach, a spa town east of Trier, where they had moved to escape her unkind relations. Soon after Marx had visited her there in March to plan the wedding she wrote to him: 'I did not know how dear you were to me in my deepest heart until I no longer saw you in the flesh; I have only the faithful portrait of you standing so full of life before my soul in all its angelic mildness and goodness, heightened love and spiritual lustre.' Theirs was a love to endure the worst hardships of time, which it would need to be.

They were married in the Protestant Church and registry office in Kreuznach on 19 June 1843. The only members of either family present were Jenny's mother and brother Edgar. The newlyweds spent an idyllic honeymoon of several weeks in Switzerland and the province of Baden, before returning to Kreuznach. For the next three months they lived with Jenny's mother, while Marx concentrated on writing for the new review.

It was to be called the *Franco-German Annals (Deutsch-Französische Jahrbücher)*. As it was to have a political flavour, Marx set to work on an article concerning Hegel's political philosophy as set out in his *Philosophy of Right*. Hegel had thought the Prussian Government represented the ideal 'rational state', the end-result of the evolution of history. To prove it false, Marx formulated his *Critique of Hegel's Philosophy of Right*. He was still polishing it up long after the *Franco-German Annals* ceased to exist, and it was never published in his lifetime.

Two factors influenced Marx's view of Hegel's politics. First, his experience as editor of the *Rhenish Gazette* had taught him that 'legal relations as well as forms of state are to be understood neither in themselves nor from the so-called general development of the human mind', as Hegel had thought, 'but rather have their roots in the material conditions of life'. The other factor was his reading of Ludwig Feuerbach's *Preliminary Theses for the Reform of Philosophy*. He had already read Feuerbach's major work, *The Essence of Christianity*, which claimed that religious beliefs arose from alienated human desires, but it had impressed him far less than it had, among others, Friedrich Engels. But the *Theses* had an immediate impact on him. In them, Feuerbach turned Hegel's philosophy upside-down, claiming that Universal Mind was simply the essence of humanity which Hegel had mistakenly placed outside human beings and so served to alienate man from himself. Feuerbach placed at the heart of his philosophy not God, not Mind, but Man; he endeavoured to bring Hegel, whom he thought was the last bastion of theology, down to earth.

This theory gave Marx the foundation he needed to reverse Hegel's dialectic. From now on, he would have no doubt that the motive force of history was not Mind - it was Man. Feuerbach's *Theses* seemed to him to be flawed only in that they gave too much importance to nature and too little to politics. So he remedied that in his own work, giving it an added social and historical dimension, and set about demolishing Hegel's political philosophy. Citing examples of actual political institutions, he showed that Hegel's conception of the relation between ideas and reality was erroneous. Hegel had believed that reality was the unfolding of an idea, but Marx demonstrated the opposition of ideals to reality in the real world, revealing that Hegel's philosophy was speculative, i.e. based on subjective notions that disagreed with empirical reality.

Meanwhile, Ruge was trying to drum up contributors for the *Franco-German Annals*. Most of the German liberal writers refused, and in the end he was left with only the hard core of those already associated with the publisher. These were Hess, the poet Georg Herwegh, the Russian anarchist Michael Bakunin, and Engels. They had little in common except a wish for the political application of Feuerbach's philosophy; but Feuerbach himself would have nothing to do with them, as he thought the time to put his theory into practice had not yet come.

One of the few things on which the review's contributors actually agreed was that Paris, 'The Capital of Liberty', was the place to be. France was a hotbed of socialism, with a wide variety of undercover sects in existence during the decline of Louis Philippe's bourgeois monarchy.

Ruge had foreseen no problems in engaging French socialists to write for the *Franco-German Annals*. For one reason or another, they proved unwilling or unavailable, with the result that the first, misnamed edition contained not one French contribution. Still, Paris was the place to be, and Marx duly arrived in October 1843 with Jenny, who was already four months pregnant. Their first lodging was with the Ruges at 23 rue Vaneau, in the St Germain area of the Left Bank where there were many German immigrants. Ruge had rented two floors of this house, next door to the 'office' of the review at No.22, with the aim of setting up an experiment in community living, involving himself and his wife, the Marxes and two other families. It was a hapless idealistic dream. None of the families could tolerate the others, and the Marxes were relieved to move, within two weeks, to No.31. In December they settled at No.38, their home for the rest of their stay in Paris.

The first of Marx's pieces for the *Franco-German Annals* was an essay called 'On the Jewish Question', reviewing two articles by Bruno Bauer on the issue of civil and political rights for Jews. He disagreed with Bauer that the matter was a question of religion, and concentrated instead on the everyday nature of Jews, whose 'jealous god' was Money. The Jew represented 'civil society's Judaism', i.e. the social dominance of bargaining and all financial interests. The way to solve the 'Jewish question', then, was to re-organise society so as to abolish bargaining. This essay was a landmark in that, for the first time, Marx saw economic life, not religion, as the major form of human alienation. It has also given rise to an idea that Marx was anti-Semitic. But his objection to the Jews was more on the grounds of the vulgar capitalism associated with them than their religion in particular (he hated all religions) or the peculiarity of their race.

His second article for the review reflected his discovery in Paris of the class whose cause he was to champion till his death: the 'proletariat'. He saw working men at close quarters for the first time, and he was impressed by their sense of comradeship, by what he saw as the reality among them of the 'brotherhood of man', and the nobility that 'shines forth upon us from their toil-worn bodies'. His closest contacts among the workers were naturally the German immigrant artisans, and he forged especially strong links with the most radical of their secret societies, the League of the Just, which wanted to make Germany a social republic. The article 'Towards a *Critique* of Hegel's Philosophy of Right: Introduction' had all the elements of his earlier *Critique*; the difference lay in a shift of emphasis to the proletariat as the destined emancipator of society. He referred to it as 'a class with radical chains, a class in civil society that is not a class of civil society...that has a universal character because of its universal sufferings... In a word, it is the complete loss of humanity and this can only recover itself by a complete redemption of humanity. This dissolution of society, as a particular class, is the proletariat.'

The two articles appeared in the first, and only, double number of the *Franco-German Annals*, published in February 1844. The review was doomed from the start. It was instantly banned in Prussia, and met with little success in France. After the publisher had pulled out of the venture the final nail in its coffin was hammered home by the divergent views of Marx and Ruge. By this time Marx had adopted the term 'communism' as a vague description of his views, and this turned Ruge, who hated communists, completely against him. Moreover, Marx's articles were too stylish for his co-editor's liking, and the whole thing fell apart when Ruge failed to pay Marx for them. Marx might now have fallen on hard times, but he was saved by the former shareholders of the *Rhenish Gazette*, who sent him a large donation in March.

The Marxes' first daughter was born on 1 May 1844 and was named Jenny. She was a sickly baby, and her mother took her to Trier in July to consult her old doctor. There she stayed for months, while Marx, left alone, plunged into a period of intensive reading and note-making for his researches into economics, communism and Hegel. These documents, not published until 1932, are known as the *Economic and Philosophical Manuscripts of 1844*. The first of them comprises excerpts from the classical economists on wages, profit and rent, and Marx's thoughts on alienated labour; the second deals with the relation of capital to labour; the third is a discussion on private property, labour and communism, followed by a critique of Hegel's dialectic, a passage on production and an article on money; and the fourth summarises the final chapter of Hegel's *Phenomenology of Mind*. Altogether, the manuscripts can be regarded as the first of many drafts for a major work, only part of which eventually became Marx's magnum opus, *Capital*. The purpose of the manuscripts was to found a new world-view that would render Hegelianism and all its offshoots redundant; and it was based on Marx's two new insights, that economics was the major form of human alienation, and that the force that would liberate humanity from the economic yoke was the proletariat. On these corner-stones, the first Marxism was built.

In the manuscripts there appeared together for the first time what Engels later called the three constituent elements of Marx's thought: German idealist philosophy, French socialism and English economics. The central vision remained unchanged throughout the rest of Marx's work: man's alienation in capitalist society, and his possible emancipation through communism, in which he was master of his own destiny.

While Jenny was in Trier, Marx did much more than work feverishly on his manuscripts: he also formed by far the most important friendship of his life. In the Café de la Régence, on 28 August 1844, he again met Friedrich Engels.

Engels, born on 28 November 1820 in Barmen (now Wuppertal) near the Ruhr, came from a family of rich industrialists. His father had formed the partnership of Ermen & Engels, a cotton-spinning enterprise in Barmen and Manchester. Young Friedrich had been expected to follow in his father's footsteps, and in 1838 had gone to lodge with a clergyman's family in Bremen, to gain business experience. Desperate to break loose from his strict, fundamentalist upbringing, he was happy to do his military service near Berlin, where he came under the influence of the Young Hegelians. After his year in the army his father sent him to work in Manchester. On his way, he stopped in Cologne and paid a visit to the editor of the *Rhenish Gazette,* but Marx, having broken all ties with the Young Hegelians, whose behaviour had become clownish and shocking, received him coldly. In Manchester, Engels got to know leaders of the Chartist movement and busily gathered material for his bitter condemnation of

Paris - the Place to Be

capitalism, *The Conditions of the Working Class in England*. While travelling back to Germany he passed through Paris, and his historic meeting with a much more agreeable Marx took place.

After a long conversation in the Café, Engels lodged with Marx for the next ten days. They were immediately in harmony: Engels wrote, 'Our complete agreement in all theoretical fields became obvious.' Though their ideas were so similar, their friendship was in many ways an attraction of opposites. Marx's strength lay in his ability to grasp and express difficult abstract concepts, whereas Engels was an inveterate simplifier; Marx was happiest grappling with theory, while Engels drew his beliefs from first-hand experience of capitalism in practice. Their ways of life, too, were poles apart. Marx's study was always in a mess, he dressed carelessly, his capacity for managing his own money was non-existent. Engels was an immaculate dresser, his study was scrupulously tidy, and he was precise and business-like in his handling of money. He was also a promiscuous womaniser, refusing to be tied down by marriage; Marx, despite one aberration, was a family man, unshakeably loyal to his wife and children.

During their first ten days, Marx and Engels decided to collaborate on a pamphlet attacking Bruno Bauer, Marx's erstwhile friend, whose ideas he now roundly despised. Engels dashed off fifteen pages, about half the expected length of the pamphlet, and left in the company of Moses Hess to spread communist propaganda in the Rhineland. Marx set to work, characteristically painstakingly, on his part, laboured over it for three months, and ended up having written a book of almost 300 pages. It was published in February 1845 as *The Holy Family*, the title being an ironic reference to Bruno Bauer and his brother Edgar. Engels, astonished by its length, told Marx that 'the sovereign derision' which they accorded to the Bauers was 'in stark contrast to the considerable number of pages' they devoted to their criticism. Turgidity, of which there was much in *The Holy Family,* was an affliction that often befell Marx's most impassioned polemical writing.

Before *The Holy Family* was published Marx was driven out of Paris. The Prussian régime had stepped up its protests to the government of Louis Philippe about the subversive German communists living there. On 25 January 1845 an order was issued expelling Marx from France. On 2 February he left for Brussels, followed a few days later by Jenny.

The Coming of Communism

1845 – 1848

BELGIUM, a rapidly industrialising country, independent only since 1830, permitted greater freedom of expression than any other European nation, so it was a refuge for quite a number of political exiles. Marx was to live there for the next three years.

The little family spent the first months in Brussels in the Bois Sauvage guest house, then moved into the lodgings of the poet Freiligrath when he left for Switzerland. Finally, in May 1845, they rented a terraced house in the rue de l'Alliance in a Flemish-speaking district of the city. Jenny was pregnant again, and her mother sent her own maid, the 25-year-old Helene Demuth, to look after her. Helene, affectionately known as Lenchen, was to stay with the family till Marx's death, ever faithful, quiet and unassuming, doing nothing to provoke comment - except once.

Although Belgium was a relatively tolerant country, Marx still had trouble in acquiring a residence permit, which was granted only after he had signed a promise to abstain from all political activity. The Prussians were persisting in their efforts to extradite him, and so, in December 1845, after flirting with the idea of emigrating to America, he relinquished Prussian nationality, to remain stateless for the rest of his life.

Having sold their furniture and linen in Paris the Marxes were comfortably off, their wealth supplemented by a sizeable sum donated by old friends in the Rhineland after an appeal by Engels, who himself gave Marx the royalties from his *Condition of the Working Class in England*. Engels had also moved to Brussels, where he lived next door to the Marxes. The two families, together with Engels's other next-door neighbours, Moses Hess and his wife, and a variety of other friends, spent many happy evenings in the city's cafés. Indeed, his stay in Brussels was probably the most carefree period of Marx's life.

He was far from idle, though. He passed many hours in the municipal library, poring over books on economic and social problems, trying to understand all the workings of bourgeois society, the factors governing the process of history, and the chances of proletarian emancipation. It was during this time of intensive study that Marx fully developed the materialist conception of history. The only writings to have survived from this period are the eleven *Theses on Feuerbach*, which Engels called 'the first document in which the brilliant kernel of the new world view is revealed'.

The *Theses* were no more than brief comments to distinguish Marx's form of materialism from Feuerbach's, but because of their epigrammatic nature they have come to be among the most quoted of Marx's writings. As Engels published them in 1888, long before any of Marx's other early unpublished works appeared, they are also much misunderstood. They are the principal source of the Marxist doctrine of 'the unity of theory and practice', which has been taken to mean that men should live in accordance with the theoretical principles they embrace: for example, that socialists should share their wealth. In fact, Marx simply meant that the solution of theoretical problems was to be found in practical action. Specifically, he wanted to see the theoretical problem of history (a problem caused by economic and social, i.e. material, conditions) solved by the practice of communism.

The last of the *Theses* has become so closely identified with Marx that it was carved at the base of the monument erected to him in Highgate Cemetery in 1956: 'The philosophers have only interpreted the world in various ways; the point is, to change it'. This is usually taken to mean that revolutionary activity is the only important thing, and philosophy matters not at all. Marx's point, however, was that the solution to philosophical problems lay not in passive interpretation, but in action to change the world and resolve its inherent philosophical contradictions. Philosophy matters very much, only it must be complemented by action.

In July 1845 Marx and Engels visited England, to carry out extensive research into economics. They spent most of their six-week stay studying economic works in the Old Chetham Library in Manchester, after which they were a few days in London, where Marx was introduced to the Chartist leader George Julian Harney, and to prominent members of the German workers' organisations in the English capital. Meanwhile, Jenny was in Trier, keeping her lonely mother company. Jenny returned to Brussels in August, and in September gave birth to her second daughter, Laura.

When Marx came back from England he postponed his socio-economic studies to write a definitive critique of the Young Hegelians, whom he now heartily detested Called *The German Ideology*, it grew into a mostly turgid polemic of inordinate length. But one section, criticising Feuerbach, incorporated a clear statement of the materialist conception of history, a theory of history in which human activity, rather than thought, plays the crucial role:

> The first premise of all human history is, of course, the existence of living human beings. Thus the first fact to be established is the physical organisation of these individuals and their consequent relation to the rest of nature...Men can be distinguished from animals by consciousness, by religion or anything else you like. They themselves begin to distinguish themselves from animals as soon as they begin to produce their means of subsistence, a step which is conditioned

> by their physical organisation. By producing
> their means of subsistence men are indirectly
> producing their actual material life...Men who
> develop their material production and their
> material relationships alter their thinking and
> the products of their thinking along with their
> real existence. Consciousness does not deter-
> mine life, but life determines consciousness.

At the heart of the desert of *The German Ideology* the section on Feuerbach was an oasis of clarity and cogency; but, like so much of Marx's work, it was not published in his lifetime. Marx and Engels tried in vain throughout 1846 and 1847 to find a publisher for the book, which in the end had to be abandoned, as Marx later wrote, 'to the gnawing of the mice'. But it had served a purpose in helping Marx to work out his position with regard to the Young Hegelians and German socialists. Now he and Engels could concentrate on trying to convince various left-wing groups of the validity of their ideas, and through them to win over 'the European proletariat in general and the German proletariat in particular'. A clique of talented German exiles soon gathered admiringly around Marx, including one Wilhelm Wolff, who came to the Marxes' home direct from Silesia, where he had escaped from arrest for spreading communist propaganda among the peasantry.

In December 1846, two months after they had moved to Ixelles, a southern suburb of Brussels, the Marxes' first son, Edgar, was born. 'Musch', or 'little fly', as they called him, was a frail child whose tragic life would epitomise the sorrows that were soon to engulf the family. Marx's financial welfare had already begun to decline, and he fell to writing begging letters to his friends; but the situation improved, for the time being, in 1848, when his mother granted him a generous advance on his inheritance.

By this time Marx was taking more than a passive interest in communism. In January 1846, in flagrant contravention of his signed promise to abstain from political activity in Belgium, he had

The Coming of Communism

set up a Communist Correspondence Committee, designed to be a tool to co-ordinate the theory and practice of communism in the capitals of Europe. One of the effects of this venture was to fuel a controversy between Marx and the eminent French socialist Pierre Proudhon. Marx wrote to him in May 1846, inviting him to be the Committee's Paris correspondent. Proudhon had many reservations. He was against the idea of immediate revolutionary action, and warned of the dangers of indoctrinating people with communism, which would be as bad as any other form of indoctrination. This hesitant response displeased Marx, who allowed his fury to smoulder a while before erupting volcanically a year later with the publication of *The Poverty of Philosophy*, a polemic against Proudhon's book *The System of Economic Contradictions*, subtitled 'The Philosophy of Poverty'. The nucleus of Marx's criticism was that Proudhon failed to understand the historical development of humanity, and so resorted to eternal moral concepts such as Reason and Justice. He went on to dismember all aspects of Proudhon's analysis with devastating effect, the controversy thus inflamed continuing between the disciples of the two men for many years.

Most of the other French socialists were as reluctant as Proudhon to join the Committee, though a fairly regular correspondence with Germany was established, while close links were forged with the communist German workers in London, where the League of the Just based its Central Committee after leaving Paris in November 1846. Two months later the London branch of the Correspondence Committee sent Joseph Moll, a leader of the League, to Brussels to invite Marx to join the League. Marx was enticed by Moll's declaration that the League was planning to hold a congress in London, at which 'the critical position we had taken' (Marx wrote) 'would be adopted in a public manifesto as the doctrine of the League. Antiquated and dissident views could only be counteracted by our personal collaboration.' Before agreeing to join, Marx demanded 'that everything that encouraged a superstitious attitude to authority be banished from the Statutes of the League', and he was assured this would be so. He was the master: his word was law.

The congress took place in London from 2 - 9 June 1847. Marx was unable to go, being short of money, but Engels attended in the capacity of Paris representative. Decisions were taken to reorganise the League's democratic basis, to rename it the 'Communist League', to do away with the old conspiratorial approach, and to change its slogan from 'All Men are Brothers' (apparently on the insistence of Marx, who said there were many men whose brother he wished on no account to be) to 'Proletarians of All Countries - Unite'. It was proposed to hold the next congress in November, when a 'Confession of Faith', composed by Engels, would be discussed.

Marx was so excited by the success of the first congress that in August he turned the Brussels Correspondence Committee into a branch of the Communist League, installing himself as President. The League was still a secret society, and it was usual for branches to set up Workers' Associations as fronts for their activities. One of these was created in Brussels, starting with 37 members and growing fast, and afforded Marx an enjoyable opportunity for public debate.

At the end of November, at the urgent request of the League's Central Committee, Marx travelled with Engels to attend the next congress in person. At the headquarters of the German Workers' Educational Association, 20 Great Windmill Street, on 1 December 1847, the congress began, and debated for the next ten days. According to Engels, Marx was so persuasive that 'all opposition and doubt was at last overcome and the new principles were unanimously accepted'. The old, vaguely utopian statutes were superceded by new ones that stated the League's aims to be 'the overthrow of the bourgeoisie, the domination of the proletariat, the abolition of the old bourgeois society based on class antagonisms, and the establishment of a new society without classes and

The Coming of Communism

without private property'. At the end of the congress Marx and Engels were entrusted with the task of drawing up a manifesto to express and publicise the League's doctrines.

Years later, an account of Marx at the congress was given by Frederick Lessner:

> Marx...greatly impressed us all. He was of medium height, broad-shouldered, powerful in build, and vigorous in his movements. His forehead was high and finely shaped, his hair thick and pitch-black, his gaze piercing. His mouth already had the sarcastic curl that his opponents feared so much. Marx was a born leader of the people. His speech was brief, convincing and compelling in its logic. He never said a superfluous word; every sentence contained an idea and every idea was an essential link in the chain of his argument. Marx had nothing of the dreamer about him...I saw that Marx represented the manhood of socialist thought.

In Brussels again, Marx divided his time between giving a course of lectures to the German Workers' Educational Association and working on the Manifesto. Although Engels supplied a draft called *Principles of Communism* which Marx used for reference, and despite the fact that both their names appeared on the title page, the actual writing of the Manifesto was done entirely by Marx.

The Communist Manifesto, such a famous and influential work, is a very brief tract, only 12,000 words long, and Marx took no more than six weeks to complete it. All things considered, it is a remarkably succinct account of communist ideology and aspirations.

The first sentence, 'A spectre is haunting Europe - the spectre of Communism', seizes the reader's attention. Then, after a short introduction, the first section plunges into a description of the history of society as class society with the challenging statement, 'The history of all hitherto existing society is the history of class struggles.' (This bold assertion is easily disproved; but Marx was in no mood to admit any argument against him). He went on to prophesy the triumph of the proletariat over the bourgeoisie. It is interesting to note that for Marx the proletariat did not, as might be imagined, mean the lowest social class. He held in utmost contempt 'the "dangerous class", the social scum, that passively rotting mass thrown off by the lowest layers of old society' which 'may, here, and there, be swept into the movement by a proletarian revolution', but whose 'conditions of life... prepare it far more for the part of a bribed tool of reactionary intrigue.' In fact, his 'proletariat', which he went on perversely to call 'the lowest stratum of our present society', was composed of the artisans, who in his opinion were most likely to be moved to revolution. In other words, 'proletariat' meant just what he wanted it to mean.

The second section of the Manifesto describes the position and role of communists in the proletarian class, dismisses bourgeois objections to communism, then summarises the forthcoming revolution, the measures to be taken by the triumphant proletariat, and the nature of the new communist society. The third section criticises various other kinds of socialism, classified as reactionary, bourgeois and utopian, while the last section outlines the position of communists in relation to the existing opposition parties, and concludes with an appeal for proletarian unity. The final paragraph epitomises Marx's tone of defiant contempt:

> The Communists disdain to conceal their views and aims. They openly declare that their ends can be attained only by the forcible overthrow of all existing social conditions. Let the ruling classes tremble at a Communistic revolution. The proletarians have nothing to lose but their chains. They have a world to win. Working men of all countries, unite!

All the ideas in the Manifesto had been expressed before, especially by French socialists. The novelty lay in its powerful synthesis and relentlessly materialist approach. It should have made a

The Coming of Communism

massive impact; but its publication was totally overshadowed by the outbreak of the revolutions of 1848.

The great revolutionary tide of that turbulent year had begun the previous November in Italy, with republics declared in Naples, Turin and Florence. Meanwhile, Louis Philippe, the complacent king of France, ordered his troops to fire on unarmed demonstrators, being foolishly confident that Parisians would never revolt in winter. But they did, and in no time the King was forced to abdicate and sent into exile, and a provisional republican government was formed.

When news of the revolution reached Brussels at the end of February the Belgian government quickly adopted a tough policy to stave off the danger of similar trouble. A list of foreigners to be deported was drawn up, with Marx's name at the top. His mother had just sent him the large advance on his inheritance, and the police suspected he was using it to finance the revolutionary movement. On 3 March he was ordered to leave the country within 24 hours. The same day he received a reply from a member of the provisional French government to his request that his earlier expulsion order be revoked. It was addressed to 'Brave and loyal Marx', going on to declare that 'the soil of the French Republic is a place of refuge for all friends of freedom. Tyranny has banished you, free France opens her doors to you and all those who fight for the holy cause, the fraternal cause of all peoples.' Once more it seemed that Paris was the place to be, and Marx prepared to leave.

His stay in Belgium ended on a sour note. That night the Communist League's Central Committee met in the Bois Sauvage guest house and decided to move its headquarters to Paris and entrust Marx with discretionary powers over the whole League. At 1 a.m. the local police commissioner burst in on the meeting and arrested Marx Jenny, after attempting to secure his release, was herself arrested, as Marx complained in a letter to a Paris paper a week later, 'on the pretext of vagabondage', and imprisoned in the Town Hall. In the morning, after waiting in a cell for two hours, she appeared before the magistrate, and was not set free with her husband until his 24 hours' grace had expired, when they were forced to leave without most of their possessions. The whole family travelled to the French border under police escort and eventually reached Paris the next day, cold, miserable and tired. It was of little consolation that the affair caused widespread outrage in Brussels and the dismissal of the police commissioner concerned. But now Marx was back in Paris, in the immediate aftermath of revolution; yet he was not to stay long.

Tide of Revolution

1848 – 1849

MARX SETTLED HIS FAMILY in the Boulevard Beaumarchais, near the Place de la Bastille, and set about involving himself in the revolutionary ferment. He immediately joined the Society of the Rights of Man, one of the largest of 147 political clubs in Paris, and was active among the German immigrants. They were so excited by the thought of revolution that a German Legion was soon formed, with several thousand recruits, and started exercises on the Champ de Mars with the aim of marching on Germany. Marx disliked this idea; according to a Communist League member, 'In one of their sessions Marx developed in a long speech the theme that the February revolution should be viewed only as the superficial beginning of the European movement. In a short time here in Paris the open struggle between proletariat and bourgeoisie would break out, as did happen, in fact, in June. The victory or defeat of revolutionary Europe would depend on this struggle'.

As a vehicle for his views Marx created a German Workers' Club, which soon had around 400 members, mostly tailors and boot makers. But it was no use. On 20 March, news came of a rising in Berlin, and the Legion was galvanised into hasty action, leaving Paris on 1 April. It was indeed an enterprise of fools; as soon as it had crossed the Rhine it was virtually annihilated by government troops. But the prospect of some kind of revolution in Germany whetted the appetite of the Communist League, whose members decided they should be there. They did not march in as brazenly and stupidly as the German Legion. They slipped in unobtrusively, singly or in small groups, armed with the *Communist Manifesto* and a flysheet called *The Demands of the Communist Party in Germany*, which propounded a plan of action for a bourgeois revolution, considered by Marx to be a necessary precursor of a communist uprising in Germany. The propaganda was designed to appeal as much to the petty bourgeoisie and the peasants as to the proletariat.

Among the infiltrators was Marx himself. With a passport valid for one year he returned to his native land in April. After staying in Mainz for two days with his family and Engels, he made his way to Cologne, settling in the north of the city on 10 April. Jenny and the children spent three months in Trier until he obtained a residence permit, then joined him in Cologne and moved to No.7 Cecilienstrasse, in a narrow street of the Old City.

In Cologne the working-class movement was well under way. A Workers' Association had just been formed by Andreas Gottschalk, a leading member of the local branch of the Communist League. There seemed little need for Marx to stay in Cologne, and there were signs that he might go on to Berlin, or even stand as a parliamentary candidate in Trier. But stay in Cologne he did, and soon fell out with Gottschalk, who was a so-called 'true' socialist, having a conciliatory attitude to religion and disagreeing with the notion that a class struggle was essential.

Marx and Gottschalk did agree on one thing: that the Communist League was now largely irrelevant, its aims overtaken by events, its members dispersed and out of touch with each other. By the time Marx exercised his power to declare a formal dissolution of the League it had practically ceased to function anyway. Free of that burden for now, Marx turned his attention back to journalism and founded a new radical newspaper, the *New Rhenish Gazette (Neue Rheinische Zeitung.)* From the very start, Marx and Engels had such difficulty in raising subscriptions to

Tide of Revolution

it that Marx had to put in a large amount of his own money. The editorial board consisted entirely of old Communist League members, over whom, according to Engels, Marx exercised 'a dictatorship pure and simple', which was 'completely natural, uncontested and freely accepted. By the clarity of his vision and resoluteness of his principles he made the paper into the most famous of the revolutionary period.' Despite its name, it was conceived as a national newspaper, carrying little local news. Marx wrote for the most part about internal politics, while Engels followed events in France and England.

It had been Marx's ambition to encourage in Germany a revolutionary atmosphere such as he had found in Paris, but he soon realised this was impossible. The German uprising threatened by the action in Berlin never materialized, and the autocratic régime, while allowing the voice of liberal opposition to be heard, retained control of the army and administration. The working-class movements were more concerned to bargain for higher wages and better working conditions than to come out in open revolt. (Indeed, the satisfaction of the 'proletariat' within the established order of society, as long as it could hope for a reasonable standard of living, was something Marx constantly overlooked in his belief that its only chance of happiness lay in revolution.)

The *New Rhenish Gazette* had a programme of two main aims: 'a single, indivisible, democratic German Republic, and war with Russia which would bring the restoration of Poland', as Engels had said. Its subtitle was 'An Organ of Democracy', and it supported a 'united front' of all democratic forces. Compatible with Marx's belief that a bourgeois overthrow of the aristocracy must precede a proletarian revolution, the paper advocated universal suffrage, direct elections, the abolition of feudal dues and charges, the establishment of a state banking system, and the admission of state responsibility for unemployment. The paper's line was that capitalism, private property and class antagonism must not only continue to exist for the time being, but actually expand, which Marx thought would hasten the conditions in which the proletarian revolution could take place.

Besides editing the paper Marx was active in local politics. A Committee of Cologne Democratic Unions summoned a congress of Rhineland Democrats which convened in August and at which Marx proved to be a dominant figure. He was later described by Karl Schurz, a Bonn student and future American senator, as 'a somewhat thick-set man, with broad forehead, very black hair and beard and dark sparkling eyes' who 'was already the recognised head of the advanced socialistic school'. But what struck Schurz most was Marx's sarcasm and intolerance of all opponents: 'I have never seen a man whose bearing was so provoking and intolerable...Everyone who contradicted him he treated with abject contempt...' A more sympathetic observer was Albert Brisbane, an editor of the *New York Daily Tribune*, who saw 'behind his self-contained reserve of manner...the fire and passion of a resolute soul'.

Meanwhile, in spite of having attained a circulation of 5,000, the *New Rhenish Gazette* was in difficulties. Marx had to appear twice before a magistrate and the premises of the paper were searched after the publication of an article by him protesting about police brutality. Worst of all, his applications for Prussian citizenship were repeatedly rejected, so he could at any time be expelled as an undesirable alien.

In August 1848, in an effort to raise funds from Democratic leaders, Marx visited Berlin and Vienna. He managed to collect a reasonable amount before hurrying back to Cologne on 11 September to be caught up in a hectic fortnight's activity. On 13 September, after brutal provocation by the soldiers in the city, a public meeting was called by Wilhelm Wolff in the main square. Before a crowd of thousands a thirty-strong Committee of Public Safety was elected to represent the populace. Marx, though not at the meeting, was on the Committee with most of his staff,

Tide of Revolution

and another meeting was arranged for 17 September at Worringen, just outside Cologne. Ten thousand people flocked to hear speeches in favour of a Social-Democratic Republic, and a motion was carried that the participants 'would give life and limb for Germany' in the event of a war between Prussia and the rest of Germany. Another meeting was held on 20 September to voice support for the recent insurgents in Frankfurt, for whom the *New Rhenish Gazette* opened a subscription. But the Frankfurt rising was soon quelled and a strict administration imposed there.

The next congress of Rhineland Democrats was due to be held on 25 September, but that morning several of their leaders were arrested, while warrants were issued for the arrests of Engels, Wolff and others. Marx, on this occasion, was not a wanted man as he had not taken active part in any of the public meetings. On the contrary, he was instrumental in defusing a potentially explosive situation when he encouraged the incensed workers to calm down and avoid confrontation with the soldiers. This was because, as he wrote the next month, 'at this moment, there was no burning question to bring the people as a whole into the struggle, and every revolt must therefore fail.' But martial law was declared and the *New Rhenish Gazette* was suppressed.

The crisis passed. Martial Law was lifted on 3 October. Ten days later, having poured so much of his and Jenny's money into the paper that it became legally his own property, Marx brought out the next issue of the *New Rhenish Gazette*. It carried reports on the crisis in Vienna, where the Democrats had seized power; but the fleeing Emperor was soon reinstated by loyalist troops, and the tide began to turn against the revolutionaries of Europe.

Engels, having fled Prussia, spent October wandering through France, composing a charming travel diary in which his admiration of the peasants' way of life was offset by his disgust at their political ignorance. When he reached Switzerland he was supported by regular donations from

53

Marx, whose generosity he was to repay amply in the years ahead. Marx was now finding the *New Rhenish Gazette* harder and harder to produce. He wrote to Engels, 'I am up to my ears in work, and find it impossible to do anything detailed; moreover, the authorities do everything to steal my time.'

By December it was plain that the recent upheavals had petered out and the old order was mostly re-established. Marx came to discount the possibility of a bourgeois revolution in Germany and decided there were only two likely courses: 'either a feudal absolutist counter-revolution or a social-republican revolution'. But he saw no hope that the momentum for the latter could come from within the country; only an external shock could produce it. He said as much in his programme for 1849, published on New Year's Day:

> The liberation of Europe...is dependent on a successful uprising by the French working class. But every French social upheaval necessarily founders on the English bourgeoisie, on the industrial and commercial world-domination of Great Britain... And old England will only be overthrown by a world war, which is the only thing that could provide the Chartists, the organised party of the English workers, with the conditions for a successful rising against their gigantic oppressors... Revolutionary uprising of the French working class, world war - that is the programme for the year 1849.

That January, Engels returned to Cologne and wrote some articles on Eastern European affairs which turned out to be extremely ill-judged diatribes against 'the Slavic barbarians', suggesting horrifically that the next war should 'annihilate all these small pigheaded nations right down to their very names'. He took the simplistic view that whole races were once and for all either revolutionary or counter-revolutionary, and so either had a right to exist or no right to exist at all. Needless to say, his genocidal articles did nothing

Tide of Revolution

to enhance the reputation of Marx's paper.

During February a case brought against Marx for incitement the previous September (though he had done hardly anything) came up for trial. Marx defended himself eloquently, working into his speech an outline of the materialist conception of history, and was not only acquitted but thanked by the foreman of the jury for his helpful explanation. But he was now coming in for increasing criticism from his fellow-socialists, who felt his policies were not radical enough, that he had no genuine interest in the welfare of the poverty-stricken workers, that he was intent only on theorising and fashioning a revolution for his own glory.

Besides these rumblings of discontent he had also to cope with growing pressure on the *New Rhenish Gazette* from the military as well as the civil authorities. On one occasion, two NCOs called to ask him for the name of the author of an article reporting an officer's conviction for selling army material illegally. When, with reasoned argument, he refused, they told him 'they could "no longer hold their people back", and it would "turn out badly".' Unruffled by their threats, he saw them off with the help of an unloaded pistol sticking out of his dressing-gown pocket.

Marx's time in Cologne was running out. Perhaps foreseeing that he would soon be moving on he made the dramatic move on 15 April of breaking the ties he had previously fostered with the Democratic Association. A statement, signed by Marx and some others, read: 'We consider that the present organisation of Democratic Associations contains too many heterogeneous elements to allow of an activity profitable to the aims of the Cause. We are rather of the opinion that a closer connection between workers' associations is preferable as their composition is homogeneous; therefore, as from today, we are resigning from the Rhineland Committee of Democratic Associations.'

Immediately after this, Marx made a three-week trip through North-West Germany and Westphalia to collect money for his near-bankrupt paper. While

Karl Marx

he was in Hamburg the last revolution in Germany for many years broke out in Dresden, Baden and the Ruhr, but was quickly put down, apart from some lingering resistance in Baden. The renewed confidence of the authorities spelt the end for Marx; on 9 May he learned that he was to be expelled. A week later he was ordered to leave Prussia within 24 hours 'because of his shameful violation of hospitality'. The paper's other editors were also expelled, and the last edition of the *New Rhenish Gazette* appeared on 18 May, printed in red. On the first page was a defiant poem by Freiligrath, and a message from the editors to the Cologne workers, warning them against violence, which concluded: 'the last word of the *New Rhenish Gazette* will always and everywhere be: emancipation of the working class.' The 'Red Number' sold 20,000 copies and became something of a collectors' item.

Marx sold off the plant and machinery, all of which was his personal property, to pay debts to shareholders, staff and contributors. This left the family nothing but Jenny's silver, which they took with them in a borrowed suitcase when they left Cologne on 19 May 1849. They went first to Bingen, where Jenny spent a few days with friends, while Marx and Engels visited Frankfurt. There they tried in vain to persuade the leaders of the Left in the Frankfurt Assembly to take control of the revolutionary forces in South-West Germany. Jenny arranged to pawn her silver, then took the children to Trier, where she sadly found her mother turned hard and selfish by difficult circumstances in old age. Marx and Engels next travelled to Baden, where they had no success in trying to make the revolutionary leaders march on Frankfurt. Marx's influence in Germany had melted away; there was nothing left for him but to go elsewhere. He parted company with Engels, who joined the Baden revolutionaries as a bombardier, and made once again for Paris on 2 June. He would never settle in Germany again.

'Hellish Muck'

1849 – 1856

WHEN MARX RETURNED to Paris he was expecting a new revolution at any moment. But the provisional government had lost an election to the conservative royalists and moderate republicans, after which the radicals and socialists had attempted an abortive coup d'état. This had led to fresh repressive measures from the conservatives, which in turn caused a popular uprising in June. It had been put down, and Louis Napoleon overwhelmingly elected President in December 1848. A military dictatorship was now imminent.

Finding cholera-ridden Paris 'dismal', Marx settled in the rue de Lille near Les Invalides, under the pseudonym of M. Ramboz, and Jenny and the children joined him in July. He was desperately pleading with friends to help them out of abject poverty when, on 19 July, a police sergeant came and ordered him to leave Paris within 24 hours. He was given the choice of moving to the Morbihan district of Brittany, but scorned it as 'a disguised attempt at murder'. Buying time, he appealed to the Ministry of the Interior and gained a month's respite, but it was clear that he would have to go. On 24 August he sailed for England, little guessing it would be home for the rest of his life.

Jenny, the three children and Lenchen left Paris on 15 September when the lease on the house expired, with no choice but to follow Marx, so that the whole family was thrown together in London.

Karl Marx

They first stayed in a Leicester Square boarding House, which they soon left for a two-roomed flat at 4 Anderson Street, just off the King's Road in Chelsea. It was a fashionable area and the rent was high, but they were able to pay it for a while with the help of some money from Jenny's mother. Here Jenny gave birth to their fourth child, on 5 November 1849. His first name was Henry, but they called him 'Guido' or 'Föxchen', 'in honour of the great conspirator'.

Soon enough the money ran out and the Marxes were heavily in debt. In March 1850 they were humiliatingly evicted in front of a jeering crowd, an incident which Jenny described graphically in a letter to her friend Joseph Weydemeyer. She was feeding her sickly baby, who...

> sucked so hard that my breast was chafed and the skin cracked and the blood poured into his trembling little mouth...when our landlady came in. We had paid her 250 thalers during the winter and had an agreement to give the money in the future not to her but to her own landlord, who had a bailiff's warrant against her. She denied the agreement and demanded five pounds that we still owed her. As we did not have the money at the time...two bailiffs came and sequestrated all my few possessions - linen, beds, clothes - everything, even my poor child's cradle and the best toys of my daughters, who stood there weeping bitterly. They threatened to take everything away in two hours. I would then have to lie on the bare floor with my freezing children and my bad breast...We had to leave the house the next day. It was cold, rainy and dull. My husband looked for accomodation for us. When he mentioned the four children, nobody would take us in. Finally a friend helped us, we paid our rent and I hastily sold all my beds to pay the chemist, the baker, the butcher and the milkman who, alarmed at the sight of the sequestration, suddenly besieged me with their bills. The beds which we had sold were taken out and put on a cart. What was happening? It was well after sunset. We were contravening

> English law. The landlord rushed up to us with two constables, maintaining that there might be some of his belongings among the things, and that we wanted to make away abroad. In less than five minutes there were two or three hundred persons loitering around our door - the whole Chelsea mob. The beds were brought in again - they could not be delivered to the buyer until after sunrise next day. When we had sold all our possessions we were in a position to pay what we owed to the last farthing. I went with my little darlings to the two small rooms we are now occupying in the German hotel, 1 Leicester St., Leicester Square. There for £5 per week we were given a humane reception.

The humane reception at the German hotel lasted no more than a month. Five pounds a week was too much for the Marxes. As Jenny recounted, 'one morning our host refused to serve us our breakfast and we were forced to look for other lodgings.'

In April 1850 they found a home in two rooms at 64 Dean Street in Soho, in a house owned by a Jewish lace dealer. Here they passed a summer so miserable that Marx considered emigrating to America; but the ticket was 'hellishly expensive' and he was unaware that the Home Office was prepared to give financial aid to any refugees wanting to emigrate. In the event, prompted by the death of poor little Guido from meningitis that September, the family simply moved along the road to three rooms at 28 Dean Street, which they rented for £22 a year as sub-tenants of Morgan Kavanagh, an Irish author. Here they spent the next six years.

Despite the hardships that now beset him, Marx retained an active interest in politics. For the first few months in London he was busy on behalf of the refugees in conjunction with the German Workers' Educational Association, reorganising the Communist League, which had lately been revived, and trying to start a paper on the lines of the *New Rhenish Gazette*. He was able to do all this because, though he held it in the utmost contempt, the British Government was on the whole more tolerant of him and his fellow-exiles than any other under which he had lived. The Home Office rebuffed the Prussian complaint that 'members of the Communist League...discussed even regicide', with the statement that 'under our laws, mere discussion of regicide...does not constitute sufficient grounds for the arrest of the conspirators.' So, apart from occasional visits from Prussian police agents, Marx was left more or less to his own devices.

In March 1850 he brought out the first edition of a newspaper called the *New Rhenish Gazette - Political - Economic Review*. Conceived as a natural continuation of his old one, its tone was too intellectual for it to have any wide appeal, and after various wrangles with the Hamburg publisher Marx closed it down in November.

Soon after his arrival in London he had been elected president of the Central Committee of the resuscitated Communist League. But there was little harmony on the Committee as, throughout 1850, tension grew between him and August Willich, a flamboyant ex-Prussian officer who had hardly endeared himself to the Marxes by bursting in on them with insensitive exuberance early one morning when he arrived in London. After being opposed by Marx on his suggestion that the Committee should form a united front with other democratic refugee organisations, Willich took his case to a general meeting of the League, where he won the support of the majority. He was so impassioned at the next Committee meeting on 1 September that he challenged Marx to a duel. Marx wisely declined, but the gauntlet was taken up on his behalf by Conrad Schramm. The duel took place in Ostend, as it would have been illegal in England. First reports suggested that Schramm had been killed, but a day later he turned up at the Marxes' home, his head bandaged, having received only a glancing shot.

There could be no reconciliation between Marx and Willich. Resigning his post, Marx advised that the Central Committee be moved to Cologne, since the split made leadership from London

'Hellish Muck'

impossible. His advice was taken, and thereafter he took no further interest in the League until May 1851, when the Cologne Committee members were arrested. At the trial the prosecution fabricated evidence to connect them and Marx with the Willich faction's wild conspiracies in Paris. Marx created a committee to collect money for the defendants and organised letters of protest to British newspapers. Although he succeeded in exposing the prosecution's lies most of the accused were convicted anyway. Soon afterwards, having collapsed in Germany, the Communist League was fully dissolved on Marx's recommendation. For the next decade he belonged to no political party, although he remained a close and often acid observer of the affairs and intrigues of the London refugees, Willich among them.

In June 1850 Marx had made an important advance by acquiring a ticket to the Reading Room of the British Museum, where he was to spend so much time, studying, as tradition has it, at seat number 07. In the next three months he perused mostly back numbers of *The Economist*, from which he concluded, according to Engels, that 'the industrial prosperity, which had been returning gradually since the middle of 1848...was the revitalising force of the newly-strengthened European reaction.'

During the years at Dean Street, though, world affairs took second place to family ones. They lived in poverty and squalor, their situation not helped by the birth, on 28 March 1851, of another child, Franziska, whose pathetic life lasted just over a year, until she succumbed to broncho-pneumonia on 14 April 1852. 'When she died,' wrote Jenny, 'we left her lifeless little body in the back room, went into the front room and made our beds on the floor. Our three living children lay down by us and we all wept for the little angel whose livid, lifeless body was in the next room.'

There was another addition to the crowded household in June 1851, when the faithful Lenchen, described by Wilhelm Liebknecht as 'nice looking with rather pleasing features', gave birth to

61

a son, Frederick, whose father unquestionably was Marx. All reference to the scandal was eliminated from the Marx papers, and only quite recently did it come to light through the chance discovery of a letter. Engels, who must have had so many illegitimate children that one more made no difference, accepted paternity, and the boy was sent off to foster-parents, never to have contact with the Marx household until getting in touch with his mother after Marx's death. But Jenny knew all about it. It was only their profound love and the need to keep up appearances that sustained their marriage. Her own health was deteriorating by now, and the nervous strain of this affair can only have made her worse.

In February 1852 Marx was forced to pawn his last coat, while in April he had to borrow money to bury Franziska. In September he wrote,

> My wife is ill, little Jenny is ill, Lenchen has a sort of nervous fever, I cannot and could not call the doctor because I have no money for medicine. For 8 - 10 days I have fed the family on bread and potatoes of which it is still questionable whether I can rustle up any today...The best and most desirable thing that could happen would be that the landlady throw me out of the house. At least I would then be quit of the sum of £22. But I can scarcely trust her to be so obliging. Also baker, milkman, the man with the tea, greengrocer, old butcher's bills. How can I get clear of all this hellish muck?

To a large extent Marx brought poverty on himself by his total inability to manage money. He was fortunate to have generous and devoted friends, greatest among them the indispensable Engels, who, with a regular income since rejoining Ermen & Engels in Manchester in November 1850, was able and willing to rescue Marx time and again. The correspondence between the two friends was colossal. Throughout the twenty years from 1850 they wrote to each other on average every other day. Engels sent his donations either in postal orders or in £1 or £5 notes, cut in half and sent in separate envelopes, and Marx knew he would never fail. Once, according to Jenny, 'Karl was frightfully happy when he heard the fateful double knock of the postman. "There's Frederick, £2, saved!" he cried out.'

The environment in which Marx existed was described by a Prussian police agent who visited him in 1852:

> In the whole apartment there is not one clean and solid piece of furniture. Everything is broken, tattered and torn, with a half inch of dust over everything...When you enter Marx's room smoke and tobacco fumes make your eyes water so much that for a moment you seem to be groping about in a cavern, but gradually, as you grow accustomed to the fog, you can make out certain objects...Here is a chair with only three legs, on another chair the children are playing at cooking...

The same agent gave this account of Marx himself:

> In private life he is an extremely disorderly cynical human being, and a bad host. He leads a real gypsy existence. Washing, grooming and changing his linen are things he does rarely, and he is often drunk. Though he is often idle for days on end, he will work day and night with tireless endurance when he has a great deal of work to do. He has no fixed times for going to sleep and waking up. He often stays up all night, and then lies down fully clothed on the sofa at midday and sleeps till evening, untroubled by the whole world coming and going through the room.

There was occasional relief from the hard grind of poverty. Often on Sundays the family went for picnics on Hampstead Heath, armed with a huge lunch-basket, discussing politics and indulging in games and donkey-riding. Marx also escaped now and then for evenings out with his friends, on one occasion going on a memorable 'beer trip' of all the bars along the Tottenham Court Road, ending up by smashing several street lamps. This drew chase from several policemen, who were eluded when Marx and his friends ducked into an alley and doubled back.

But these were rare interludes in a life of rare misery. Jenny was often confined to bed, emaciated and coughing, taking port and brandy that seemed only to make her worse. Marx was driven to such despair that he wrote, 'When I see the sufferings of my wife and my own powerlessness I could rush into the devil's jaws.' Quite apart from the emotional anguish it caused him her ill-health also held up his work, as she often went to meetings, and read newspaper articles for him, and was invaluable at writing letters and making fair copies of his articles from handwriting legible only to her. He drove her too hard but she loved to help, recalling later: 'The memory of the days I spent in his little study copying his scrawled articles is among the happiest of my life.' But her temperament, as Marx was fond of saying, was 'mercurial', and the strain of so much work told heavily on her nerves.

For all the horrors of Dean Street, Marx did somehow manage to do a fair amount of work. In 1852 he responded to Louis Napoleon's seizure of power as Emperor of France by writing *The Eighteenth Brumaire of Louis Bonaparte*, the title referring to the date, in the French Revolutionary Calendar, of the first Napoleon's similar coup d'état in 1799. In this penetrating work Marx examined the socio-political background to Louis Napoleon's coup, showing 'how the class struggle in France created circumstances and relationships that made it possible for a grotesque mediocrity to play a hero's part.'

He also spent many hours in the quiet haven of the British Museum, continuing his economic studies. These convinced him that an essential precondition of any revolution was a commercial and financial crisis. Right up to 1856 he was constantly predicting its outbreak, was constantly

'Hellish Muck'

wrong, yet constantly undaunted, to the amusement of his friends. He was not too sad as the prospects of such a crisis receded, however, for it gave him more breathing space to tackle his great work on economics. He read the classical economists voraciously, but the task of actually writing the book proved beyond him for the moment, and he shelved the project in 1852.

In April that year, shortly before his thirty-fourth birthday, he had returned to journalism, with a job that provided his only regular income during his time at Dean Street. He had been invited in 1851 to write for the *New York Daily Tribune* by its socialist editor Charles Dana. Marx's first commission was for a series of articles on German current affairs, a task which, as his command of written English was still poor, he handed over to Engels. He asked for 'witty and straightforward' pieces, and the compliant Engels obliged with eighteen articles that were published under Marx's name and long thought to be his work. On the strength of them Marx was offered a regular post, and from 1852 to 1856 contributed his own articles, with mere assistance from Engels now and then. The *Tribune* published them frequently at first, but the number that appeared dwindled year by year. Marx continued to write for the paper until 1862, when Dana told him to send no more pieces as the Civil War was taking up all the space. In all, 487 articles from Marx had been published in the paper, 350 actually by him, 125 by Engels and 12 by the two of them in collaboration. They also submitted 67 others, dealing mostly with Engels's forte, military history, to the *New American Cyclopaedia*, the project of Dana's friend George Ripley. Marx had a low regard for his work for the *Tribune*, but, even at its worst, his journalism was perceptive, and it brought in at least a little money.

No money could soften the pain of the most shattering blow, which came towards the end of that hellish time in Dean Street. On 16 January 1855, after 'approaching the catastrophe with firm steps', according to Marx, Jenny gave birth

65

to another daughter, Eleanor (later affectionately known as Tussy). This was bad enough: another mouth to feed, the new baby screaming all the time, Jenny too sick to feed her herself, so that a wet-nurse was needed; but the worst was to come three months later. All through March eight-year-old Edgar, 'little fly', the apple of his father's eye, was ill with a kind of consumption. He had never known good health; Liebknecht called him 'very gifted, but ailing from the day of his birth - a genuine, true child of sorrow this boy with the magnificent eyes and promising head that was, however, made too large for the weak body.' Nothing could be done to save him; and on Good Friday, 6 April, he died in Marx's arms. Liebknecht saw 'the mother silently weeping, bent over the dead child, Lenchen sobbing beside her, Marx in a terrible agitation vehemently, almost angrily, rejecting all consolation, the two girls clinging to their mother crying quietly, the mother clasping them convulsively as if to hold them and defend them against Death that had robbed her of her boy.'

This was the last tragedy of Dean Street. In 1856 the Marxes' financial troubles were eased when Jenny inherited about £150 in May from a Scottish uncle and about £120 after the death of her mother in July. In September they moved; and they were not sorry to leave.

Poverty, Illness - and 'Capital'

1856 – 1864

THEIR NEW HOME was 9 Grafton Terrace, Kentish Town: 'a small house at the foot of romantic Hampstead Heath, not far from lovely Primrose Hill', wrote Jenny. The narrow, terraced building, in the middle of a new development area, had three storeys and a basement, eight rooms in all. It was a mean enough dwelling; but for Jenny, at first, it was heaven. She wrote: 'When we slept in our own beds for the first time, sat on our own chairs and even had a parlour with second-hand furniture of a rococo style - or rather bric-a-brac, then we really thought that we were living in a magic castle...' But the castle was at the heart of a wasteland of sticky red soil that turned into a quagmire in wet weather, with no made-up road to the house, and building going on all around. The sudden shock of an isolated life, cut off from the city's bustle, was particularly severe for Jenny, who missed the walks, the meetings, the conversations that took her mind off poverty, which was ever present. After using the inheritances to pay off old debts and set up the house, Marx had not enough left even for the first quarter of the yearly rent of £36.

In 1857 the economic crisis he had so long foretold actually happened. It made him frantic to finish off his economic studies, 'working madly through the nights', and he was soon taking a long course of medicine, having 'overdone my night-time labours, which were accompanied on the

67

Karl Marx

one side only by a glass of lemonade but on the other by an immense amount of tobacco'. He had begun the synthesis of his studies in August with a 30-page General Introduction, discussing the problem of method in studying economics and trying to justify the unhistorical order of the sections of the main work. The surviving manuscripts of this work, written between October 1857 and March 1858, have become known as *Outlines of a Critique of Political Economy*, or *Grundrisse* (the German for 'Outlines'). The plan for the work was ambitious, covering the whole range of economics, broadly simplified in a later plan in the Preface to the *Critique of Political Economy* of 1859: 'Capital, landed property, wage-labour; state, foreign trade, world market'. But the *Grundrisse* is no more than a draft for the first section, divided into two parts, on money and capital. It marks the culmination of Marx's thought begun in the *1844 Manuscripts*; in it, most of the elements of his philosophy are at least suggested: communal production in which the quality of work determines its value; the disappearance of money and of exchange-value; and an increase in leisure time, providing opportunities for the universal development of the individual.

By March 1858 he had compiled 800 manuscript pages in a furious burst of creative effort, and had only to find a publisher. One in Germany was willing to bring it out in a series of short volumes; but Marx, suffering from a liver complaint and anxious about financial problems, was unable to work up even the first section into publishable form.

Engels had imagined the Marxes to have escaped poverty forever when they moved to Grafton Terrace, so he was surprised to hear from Marx now that 'I am living a precarious existence...I have no prospects and growing family expenses... In fact I am in a more parlous situation than five years ago...' Engels promised him £5 a month to supplement his falling income from the *New York Daily Tribune*. But in July 1858 the position was even worse. Marx told Engels: 'I am completely disabled as far as work goes, partly because I lose

Poverty, Illness - and 'Capital'

most of my time in useless running around trying to make money and partly (perhaps as a result of my feeble physical condition) because my power of intellectual concentration is undermined by domestic problems. My wife's nerves are quite ruined by the filth...' The doctor advised Jenny to go to the seaside to avoid an inflammation of the brain, but even that would be no use 'if', said Marx, 'the spectre of an inevitable and ultimate catastrophe pursues her'. He enclosed a list of his debts, composed by Jenny, saying, 'I have now made a clean breast of it and I can assure you that it has cost me no little effort...I would not wish upon my bitterest enemy to wade through the quagmire in which I have been sitting for the last eight weeks...' Engels promptly sent £60, and Marx could breathe again.

He returned to the task of preparing his work for publication. After being delayed by the nagging illness of the liver he had the manuscript ready in January 1859, though it was not as he had intended it. He had originally been adamant that the part on capital 'must appear simultaneously. The inner consistency makes it necessary and the whole effect depends on it.' But the manuscript, as submitted to the publisher, contained absolutely nothing on capital. It was eventually, after further difficulties, published in June 1859 as a *Critique of Political Economy*. In the Preface, Marx gave a famously succinct account of the materialist conception of history: 'legal relations as well as forms of state are to be grasped neither from themselves nor from the so-called general development of the human mind, but rather have their roots in the material conditions of life...' But the following work was very fragmentary and was poorly received by even his closest friends. Reaction in Germany was non-existent, the worst possible thing for Marx, who would have relished 'attacks or criticisms', anything other than disregard.

Whatever hope he entertained of finishing his great work was shattered now by a quarrel with Karl Vogt, an essentially trivial matter concerning Vogt's support of Louis Napoleon in the Franco-Austrian War. This absorbed Marx for eighteen months, his efforts culminating in the publication at the end of 1860 of *Herr Vogt*, a long book which Marx called 'a system of mockery and contempt'. Jenny found it amusing, Engels thought it better than the *Eighteenth Brumaire*, but the public was uninterested and the book failed dismally. The whole affair was just a waste of time and a needless hindrance to Marx's more important work.

At the beginning of 1861, rid of the Vogt affair, Marx began to consider returning to Prussia. A political amnesty had just been declared by the new King Wilhelm I, and Ferdinand Lassalle suggested a revival of the *New Rhenish Gazette*, financed by his wealthy patron, the Countess von Hatzfeld. Lassalle was the son of a Jewish tailor and seven years Marx's junior, a socialist with whom Marx already had a stormy relationship, now friendly, now hostile. Marx was sceptical of the project and reluctant to work with Lassalle, but went to Berlin anyway to discuss the prospects and seek Prussian nationality. He set off in February 1861, stopping in Zaltbommel for a two-week stay with his Dutch uncle, Lion Philips, whom he coaxed into lending him an advance on his mother's estate of £160.

In Berlin, Lassalle entertained him in grand style for three weeks, with visits to the theatre and ballet, and a dinner held in Marx's honour. But he was soon bored with the torpid city, where there was hardly any political activity and where he was 'treated as a sort of lion and compelled to meet many professionally "intellectual" ladies and gentlemen'. He liked the idea of bringing out a new paper, but could not agree to Lassalle's terms, which in his opinion gave the latter too much power. He left Berlin, loaded down with splendid gifts for the family from Lassalle, though without Prussian nationality. On the way home, he visited his mother in Trier, and was fascinated by her 'subtle ésprit and indestructible stability of character'; she was also mellowed enough to cancel some of his old debts. Back in London, he decided he would rather not live in Germany, especially Berlin 'with its dust and culture and over-clever people'.

Now he plumbed new depths of domestic misery.

Poverty, Illness - and 'Capital'

It was a curious paradox of Marx's character that, while he despised the bourgeoisie and all its values, he was determined at all times to maintain a dignified appearance in bourgeois society. So, now that the family was living in a more respectable area, there were more appearances to be kept up. The elder daughters were attending a 'ladies' seminary', and having private lessons in French, Italian, drawing and music. There was also a second maid, Lenchen's younger sister Marianne, who came in 1857 and stayed till her death in 1862. Marx was still determined to 'pursue my aim through thick and thin and not let bourgeois society turn me into a money-making machine', an attitude that brought financial problems which caught him by surprise. In September 1859 Engels had for once been unable to help, as he was being sued for damages after assaulting someone with his umbrella, and Marx had had to turn to Lassalle. Next year was a little better, as Engels's finances were improving and he sent Marx £100 in a lump sum. A lot of the money was wasted on the Vogt affair, and by the end of the year Engels was borrowing in order to save his friend.

The worst year was 1862. Jenny even tried to sell some of Marx's books, and he had just returned in July from several weeks' hiding in Manchester to avoid creditors when Lassalle paid him a return visit. He stayed for three weeks, during which time, Marx told Engels, 'in order to preserve a certain façade, my wife had to take to the pawnbrokers everything that was not actually nailed down.' Marx came to loathe Lassalle, who had just tossed away £100 in speculation and was spending over £1 a day on cards and cigars, who offered to take one of the Marxes' daughters as a 'companion' for the Countess, and who assumed that Marx, working frantically on his 'Economics', was unemployed and so had plenty of time to spend with him. Marx was infuriated by Lassalle's arrogant bragging about his own brilliance; but when, on the day Lassalle was leaving, Marx was threatened by the landlord and other creditors with reprisals unless he paid his debts, Lassalle lent him £60.

Karl Marx

Marx failed to appreciate this act of generosity, as Lassalle wanted assurances that Engels would guarantee the loan. Marx answered him roughly, and did not apologise for his ingratitude until November.

Lassalle went on campaigning for socialism in Germany, but not along lines of which Marx approved. In May 1863 he founded the General Union of German Workers (ADAV), the first German socialist party, but only after having negotiations with Bismarck. Whether he had sold out to Bismarck, as Marx suspected, never became clear, for Lassalle was killed in a duel on 28 August 1864. For all their differences, Marx was saddened by his death; he wrote that Lassalle 'was after all one of the old stock and the enemy of our enemies...The devil knows, the crowd is getting ever smaller and no new blood is being added.'

In the autumn of 1862 Marx was reduced, for the first and only time in all his 33 years in London, and at the age of 44, to looking for work. He was rejected for a job in a railway office because of his atrocious handwriting. In January 1863, he told Engels that his troubles had 'at last brought my wife to agree to a suggestion that I made a long time ago and which, with all its inconveniences, is not only the sole solution, but is also preferable to the life of the last three years...I will write to all my creditors...and say that, if they do not leave me in peace I will declare myself bankrupt...My two eldest daughters will get positions as governesses... Lenchen will enter another service and I, with my wife and Tussy, will go and live in the City Model Lodging House.' Engels, reading this as a desperate plea, instantly borrowed £100 and sent it to him, following it up in the summer with a further £250. This tided Marx over until December, when a telegram came that spelt lasting relief: his mother had died.

He rushed to Trier. Execution of the will was delayed, so he went to see his uncle, the executor, in Zaltbommel. While in Trier, he had been pleased to be 'asked daily, left and right, after the former "prettiest girl in Trier" and the "queen of the ball". It is damned pleasant for a man when his

Poverty, Illness - and 'Capital'

wife lives on like that in the imagination of a whole city as an "enchanted princess".'

While he waited for the legal processes to be completed, Marx was afflicted with a massive carbuncle that kept him in Zaltbommel for six weeks, being nursed by his uncle and cousin Antoinette Philips. This he considered 'one of the happiest episodes of my life'; meanwhile, Engels paid the bills for Grafton Terrace. When Marx eventually came home on 19 February 1864 he brought with him the bulk of his inheritance of about £1,000. In May, he had an unexpected bonus when Wilhelm Wolff died. Though a close friend, Marx had no idea that Wolff had accumulated a small fortune, and was staggered to find that he had been left most of it, nearly £900. This double windfall should have put an end to the Marxes' financial worries, and so it did - for just over a year.

The member of the family who had been worst affected by the constant stream of financial disasters was Jenny, whose health had suffered fearfully. In 1856, aged 42, she had given birth to a still-born child after a pregnancy that almost reduced her to a nervous wreck. The next year she had gone with Lenchen and the children to Ramsgate for some weeks to recuperate, and this had become an annual event; the Marxes were great believers in the healthy properties of sea air.

As Jenny's health disintegrated, so did her optimism and joie de vivre. The turning-point in her life had come in November 1860 when, despite a double vaccination, she contracted smallpox. The children were sent to stay with the Liebknechts, and Marx hired a nurse for Jenny, who had lost the use of her senses. She wrote later: 'I lay constantly by the open window so that the cold November air would blow over me, while there was a raging fire in the stove and burning ice on my lips, and I was given drops of claret from time to time. I could hardly swallow, my hearing was getting weaker, and finally my eyes closed, so that I did not know whether I would remain enveloped in eternal night.' Meanwhile, Marx only kept hold of his 'quietness of mind' by engrossing himself in the study of mathematics.

By Christmas the worst was over and the children came home. Jenny remained rather deaf and was scarred with red pocks that healed very slowly. She wrote that before the smallpox she 'had had no grey hair and my teeth and figure were good...But that was all a thing of the past now and I seemed to myself now a kind of cross between a rhinoceros and hippopotamus whose place was in the zoo rather than among the members of the Caucasian race.'

As Jenny became more morose, Marx found it necessary to play the silent stoic, a role to which he was hardly accustomed. He too was suffering, from loneliness and ill-health. He needed a confidant, and unburdened his heart in his letters to Engels, continually complaining of problems with his liver, of toothache, headaches and disorders of the eyes and nerves for which he needed vast amounts of medicine. When he wrote 'such a lousy life is not worth while living' it can have been no exaggeration.

As if his troubles at home were not enough, Marx now had the only real quarrel of his life with Engels. On 6 January 1863 Mary Burns, who had lived with Engels for twenty years and whom he regarded as his wife, died. On hearing of this, Marx wrote that 'the news of Mary's death both surprised and shocked me very much. She was very good-natured, witty and devoted to you', and went straight on to give a long account of his financial troubles. A few days later Engels replied coldly: 'All my friends, including philistine acquaintances, have shown me on this occasion... more sympathy and friendship than I could expect. You found the moment suitable to enforce the superiority of your cold thought processes.' Marx apologised after ten days, pleading that he had written 'under the impression of very desperate conditions', and that 'in such circumstances, I can generally save myself only by cynicism.' Engels accepted this, and harmony was restored.

Poverty, Illness - and 'Capital'

The children were another cause of concern for the Marxes. Jenny found poverty all the worse because 'the sweet girls...have to suffer it as well'. In 1863, when they were nineteen, eighteen and eight, she described them: 'All three of them look very neat and interesting. Jennychen is strikingly dark in hair, eyes and complexion and, with her childishly rosy cheeks and deep, sweet eyes, has a very attractive appearance. Laura, who is in everything a few degrees lighter and clearer, is in fact prettier than the eldest sister as her features are more regular and her green eyes under her dark brows and long lashes shine with a continual fire of joy...The third one, the baby, is a true bundle of sweetness, charm and childish frenzy. She is the light and life of the house...' Indeed, it was only the tomboy exuberance of Eleanor that helped to keep Marx buoyant in the darkest times.

It was against this backdrop of poverty, illness and frayed nerves that Marx struggled to write what was to become *Capital*. He had set to work in earnest in the summer of 1861, making slow progress for a year as he tried to popularise his style. By June 1862 he was 'working like the devil', although becoming overwhelmed by depression as the domestic problems piled up. But by the end of 1862 he could say that 'the second part is now at last finished', containing 'only what was intended as the third chapter of the first part, i.e. "Capital in General"...It is (together with the first bit) the quintessence, and the development of what follows would be easy to complete, even by others, on the basis of what exists...' But it still needed copying and polishing. Marx was too ill to manage this in the spring of 1863; but by the summer he was working ten hours a day. Then, in the autumn, the boils struck.

They came out of the blue and almost killed him. 'On 10 November', wrote Jenny, 'a terrible abscess was opened and he was in danger for a fairly long time afterwards. The disease lasted a good four weeks and caused severe physical sufferings. These were accompanied by rankling moral tortures of all kinds.' During the operation, Jenny had to leave the room, while Lenchen held down Marx, who amazed the doctor with his grim stoicism. Though he recovered, he had not experienced the last of the boils. They kept recurring constantly, year after year, usually starting in autumn and reaching maturity in January. At times his body was so covered with them that he could only stand erect or lie on his side on the sofa to avoid agony. He took such bizarre medicines as creosote, opium and arsenic, gave up smoking for months and had daily cold baths, all to no avail. He researched the subject of boils so deeply in the British Museum that eventually he claimed to know more about them than any doctor. In dire necessity, he would even operate on himself. 'I always recognise what is necessary,' he told Engels. 'Today, I took a sharp razor...and cut the wretch in my own person.' There was only one consolation: it was a 'truly proletarian disease'.

Through it all he pressed on with his work. Though not finally published until 1867, *Capital*, Volume One, was mostly written during this period in such extreme conditions of poverty and pain.

It is a work in two distinct parts. The first nine chapters, containing 'the general abstract definitions which are more or less applicable to all forms of society', are difficult to read, partly because of their very abstraction, partly because Marx employed what he called the 'rational kernel' of the 'mystical shell' of the Hegelian dialectic, and partly because he used concepts familiar to mid-nineteenth-century economists but since abandoned. His aim was to analyse the capitalist system in terms of 'the birth, life and death of a given social organism and its replacement by another, superior order.'

These nine chapters divide into three parts. The first, a rewriting of the 1859 *Critique of Political Economy*, analyses commodities and their values. Two kinds of value are postulated: use-value, or the utility of something, and exchange-value, decided by the amount of labour put into the commodity. The next part concerns the transformation of money into capital; and the third brings in

Poverty, Illness - and 'Capital'

Marx's idea of surplus value, a complex theory involving the notion that a worker receives only the exchange-value, not the use-value, of his labour, and that, after working a certain time to produce the use-values of the things he needs (food, clothing, etc.), is made to work further. The time in which he produces the value of what he needs is 'necessary labour'; the extra time is a kind of forced labour, 'surplus labour', for the benefit of the capitalist, who extracts 'surplus value' from the hapless worker.

After the first nine chapters the rest of Volume One is much easier: it constitutes a compelling account of the results of capitalist efficiency. The tenth chapter, 'The Working Day', details the 'physical and mental degradation' imposed on men, women and children forced to work long hours in unhealthy conditions. More vital to the worker than any declaration of 'the inalienable rights of man' is the fight for a legally limited working day. The next chapter, 'Machinery and Modern Industry', shows how the division of labour annuls intellectual and manual skill and reduces the worker to a mere appendage of the machine. The last chapter, 'Capitalist Accumulation', describes the 'industrial reserve army' of temporarily unemployed workers, living in dire poverty, created by capitalism to keep the working 'labour army' in check.

Marx's arguments are movingly supported by detailed evidence of the recent condition of the British working class, the plight of the agricultural population, and the misery of Ireland, showing capital 'dripping from head to foot, from every pore, with blood and dirt'. Near the end, Marx proclaims that the laws of capitalism will bring about its destruction. Capitalist competition will lead to a diminishing number of monopoly capitalists, while the 'misery, oppression, slavery, degradation, exploitation' of the working class grows. But it is a class 'always increasing in numbers, and disciplined, united, organised by the very mechanism of the process of capitalist production itself.' Eventually, there will be revolution, when 'the knell of capitalist private property sounds. The expropriators are expropriated.'

Volumes Two and Three, left in draft form for Engels to polish up and publish after Marx's death, are far less interesting. Volume Two discusses the circulation of capital and the origin of economic crises, while Volume Three answers some questions raised by Volume One, concerning the disparate relation between values and prices, and Marx's idea that, under capitalism, the rate of profit tends to fall.

There is no doubt that *Capital*, especially Volume One, is Marx's masterpiece. Its predictions may not have come true; its theories may be (to say the least) contentious; but, for its presentation of the true horrors of life behind the façade of nineteenth-century capitalism, told in vivid detail and with superb style, it remains a worthwhile contribution to both history and literature. On its first publication, in Hamburg in September 1867, it did not enjoy marked success; but, gathering momentum with each new edition and each translation into another language, it has come to secure Marx his place in history.

A 'Powerful Machine'

1864 – 1872

THE 1864 INHERITANCES gave Marx the security to finish *Capital*, Volume One, but they were only a temporary solution to his problems. In April 1864, excited by sudden wealth, the family moved to a larger house, 1 Modena Villas (later to become 1 Maitland Park Road), which Jenny called 'a new, sunnily placed, friendly house with airy light rooms'. Marx's pride was his study, described by his future son-in-law, Paul Lafargue:

> It was on the first floor, flooded by light from a broad window that looked out onto the park. Opposite the window and on either side of the fireplace the walls were lined with bookcases filled with books and stocked up to the ceiling with newspapers and manuscripts. Opposite the fireplace on one side of the window were two tables piled up with papers, books and newspapers; in the middle of the room, well in the light, stood a small, plain desk (three foot by two) and a wooden armchair; between the armchair and the bookcase, opposite the window, was a leather sofa on which Marx used to lie down for a rest from time to time. On the mantelpiece were more books, cigars, matches, tobacco boxes, paperweights and photographs of Marx's daughters and wife, Wilhelm Wolff and Friedrich Engels.

The money spent on furniture came to £500, the rates and rent were almost double those of Grafton Terrace, and in October the girls gave a ball for their friends, all of which contributed to a worsening financial situation. Marx was soon writing Engels another begging letter, admitting 'it is duly crushing, to remain dependent for half of one's life. The one thought that sustains me here is that we two are executing a combined task in which I give my time to the theoretical and party political side of the business.'

Engels came to the rescue with a promise of at least £200 a year. It was still not enough. By 1866 there was the added problem of keeping up appearances for the benefit of Paul Lafargue, who was courting Laura. Finally, in November 1868, Engels could bear it no longer. He asked Marx to let him know exactly how much he needed to pay off all his debts, and whether he could manage from then on with £350 a year. Marx was 'quite knocked down', and found his total debts, listed by Jenny, 'much larger' than he had supposed. Engels let himself be bought out of the family firm, leaving joyfully on 1 July 1869, and paid everything. Only three weeks later Marx found Jenny unable to manage on her weekly allowance. It transpired, he told Engels, that 'in the list of debts...she had suppressed about £75 which she was now trying to pay off little by little from the house allowance. When I asked why, she replied that she was frightened to come out with the vast total. Women plainly always need to be controlled!' Engels gladly paid up, and the Marxes' financial troubles were over. During the last four years alone, Engels had given Marx £1,862.

Throughout this period, much time which Marx might have preferred to devote to the later volumes of *Capital* was taken up by his work for the International. He had avoided all party political commitment since 1852, keeping his head down in a time of reaction when left-wing agitation would have been unwise. But working-class activities had revived recently in a more relaxed political climate, and there was also a growing spirit of internationalism, heightened by the Polish insurrection of 1863. That July, after a mass meeting on Poland held in London and attended by a delegation of French as well as English workers, George Odger, Secretary of the London Trades Council, was engaged to write an address proposing an international association to unite the working men of all countries in peace and common fellowship. The French drafted a reply, and after the addresses had been exchanged, at a meeting at St Martin's Hall near Covent Garden on 28 September 1864, the International Working Men's Association was founded.

Marx, long interested in the Polish cause and optimistic about the effects of the 1863 insurrection, was invited to the meeting. He told Engels, 'a certain Le Lubez was sent to me to ask whether I would take part on behalf of the German workers and in particular whether I could supply a German worker to speak at the meeting. I supplied Eccarius, who was a great success, and I was also there - a silent figure on the platform. I knew that this time the real "powers" from both London and Paris sides were present, and so decided to waive my otherwise standing rule to decline any such invitations.'

Two thousand people were at the meeting. The English address and the French reply were read: the French proposed a Central Committee in London to correspond with sub-committees in the European capitals, and two British trade unionists proposed the formation of a General Committee to draw up rules for the association. After a debate this committee was elected, consisting of 27 Englishmen, three Frenchmen, two Italians, and two Germans (Marx and Eccarius).

The Committee, soon renamed the General Council, met on 5 October, when Odger was elected President. Secretaries were appointed for each country, Marx being the obvious choice for Germany. The Council, cumbrously large and full of conflicting views, not surprisingly failed to agree on a unanimous programme. Marx had already left the meeting, no doubt exasperated, when he was elected on to a sub-committee of nine to formulate a declaration of principles. Through illness, he was unable to attend the sub-committee's meetings, and the declaration was drafted without him. When he next turned up at the General Council meeting on 18 October he was 'really shocked when I heard the worthy Le Lubez read out an appallingly verbose, badly written and completely crude preamble pretending to be a declaration of principles...' It would not do; so, at the next meeting of the sub-committee, held at his home two days later, Marx contrived to debate so long that at 1 a.m. the meeting was adjourned and he was left with the papers. Briefed simply to give expression to the 'sentiments' of the approved draft, he took it upon himself to rewrite the thing entirely.

As he told Engels, he did it 'in such a way that our view appeared in a form that made it acceptable to the present standpoint of the workers' movement.' There were no rousing calls to revolution. The Address, beginning with the statement, 'It is a great fact that the misery of the working masses has not diminished from 1848 to 1864', described with the aid of quotations from official British publications the widespread poverty in England. Marx concluded that 'in all countries of Europe it has become a truth demonstrable to every unprejudiced mind...that no improvement of machinery, no application of science to production, no contrivance of communication, no new colonies, no emigration, no opening of markets, no free trade, nor all these things put together, will do away with the miseries of the industrial masses.'

On political matters, Marx noted the failure of recent European working-class movements, but pointed out the relief offered by the passing of the Ten Hours Bill and by the co-operative movement, which however could succeed over capitalism only if it grew 'to national dimensions'. After outlining various working-class achievements, he finished with the now familiar appeal: 'Proletarians of all countries, unite!'

This Inaugural Address, together with the ten

A 'Powerful Machine'

Rules concerning matters such as congresses and committee election, was approved by the General Council, though Marx was obliged to admit into the statutes some phrases on 'duty', 'right' and 'truth, morality and justice'.

Over the next six years the International grew steadily within Marx's loose doctrinal framework. It was given publicity in the *Beehive*, an influential working-class paper, and affiliations were established with several important English unions. There were annual congresses, the first in London in 1865, followed by Geneva in 1866, where the views of Marx (who attended only the last congress in 1872) were opposed by the Proudhonists; then, over the next three years, came Lausanne, Brussels and Basle. At Brussels the Proudhonist ideas were finally defeated; at Basle the Russian anarchist Bakunin made his first appearance

Though Marx was absent from all these meetings he had plenty of work to do in the General Council, and he was not best pleased about it. By the end of 1865, when he was having to pretend to be away on a journey to find time to work on *Capital*, he told Engels that 'the International and everything to do with it haunts me like a nightmare'. But he was generally on good terms with the rest of the Council, apart from occasional differences with the English, and a clash with the followers of the Italian, Mazzini, who tried to oust him at the end of 1865. Among other objections, they particularly hated the 'class' character of his ideas. Marx rallied the foreign secretaries to his side, and thwarted Mazzini's followers, who promptly left the International.

In his capacity as corresponding-secretary for Germany, Marx had little success. The ADAV, the only organised socialist party in Germany, was experiencing internal difficulties in the wake of Lassalle's sudden death, and would hardly have been receptive to Marx even if he had not been prejudiced against Lassalle's legacy. So, at first, the International's only reliable contact there was Wilhelm Liebknecht, who managed little more than to have the Inaugural Address published in the ADAV's paper before he was expelled from Prussia in July 1866. Only later that year, when the veteran socialist Becker founded active sections in a dozen German cities, did the International begin to make any impact in Germany. Nonetheless, Marx was still hopeful that the German proletariat could lead the revolutionary way, being able, as he thought, to curtail the 'bourgeois' stage of social change.

In 1867 Marx was so optimistic about the International's progress that he wrote to Engels: 'Things are moving forward, and in the next revolution, which is perhaps nearer than it seems, we (i.e. you and I) have this powerful machine in our hands...' Things were not as serene as he imagined. Fresh trouble with the English on the General Council incited him to abolish the office of President and so dispose of Odger's influence. There were also many rows with the French; and, after 1867, the International in England ground to a halt. The General Council was even evicted from its premises for debt. In Europe, however, the International continued to make strides forward, all going well until 1870, when its inner frailty became exposed. It was, in fact, only a very loose federation of national groups, each with its policies dictated largely by local rather than international interests. As such, it was not strong enough to survive the shock of the Franco-Prussian War and its aftermath.

On the outbreak of the war on 19 July 1870 the International was instantly divided. The Paris section denounced the war; the Germans were not so certain. Marx wrote an Address, in which he declared that 'the death knell of the Second Empire has already sounded at Paris', but warned that 'if the German working class allow the present war to lose its strictly defensive character and degenerate into a war against the French people, victory or defeat will prove alike disastrous.' He was sure, however, that 'the principles of the International are too widely spread and too firmly rooted amongst the German working class to apprehend such a sad consummation'. But in a Second

A 'Powerful Machine'

Address, after Prussia had adopted a more aggressive stance, he accepted the impotence of the working class 'to stop the victor amidst the clangour of arms'. National, not class, interests were prevailing, even among the workers.

Then, on 28 March 1871, the Paris Commune was formed. Louis Napoleon had abdicated and fled after the collapse of the French armies. The President, Thiers, had withdrawn all government officials to Versailles, leaving the Central Committee of the National Guard as the only body capable of control in Paris. This committee instituted direct elections which created a popular assembly, the Commune. Contrary to widespread opinion at the time, the International had nothing to do with its origins or policies; indeed, the Commune's measures were reformist rather than revolutionary.

Marx, from a distance, thought it 'the greatest achievement of our party since the June revolt'. He was also, rightly, pessimistic about the Commune's chances. At the end of May it collapsed, when between twenty and forty thousand Communards were slaughtered by government troops, the Communards for their part shooting hostages and burning buildings.

On 30 May, three days after the massacre, Marx read to the General Council an Address on the Commune (which he had been meant to have ready a month earlier) subtitled 'The Civil War in France'. This was a brilliant polemic which included an idealistic and highly subjective account of the future communist society of which Marx imagined the Commune to be the model. When published, it caused such outrage that Marx wrote to his friend Dr Kugelmann in June: 'I have the honour to be at this moment the most abused and threatened man in London. That really does me good after the tedious twenty-year idyll in my den!' But the notoriety of the Address had the more damaging effect of branding the International as the greatest menace to civilised society, and its reputation was shattered.

The last straw which broke its back was the rivalry between Marx and Bakunin. The latter's anarchist influence within the International was growing steadily. To counter it Marx called a private conference to meet in September 1871 in an inn just off the Tottenham Court Road. It was poorly attended and served only to underline the split between the Marx and Bakunin factions. Marx still clung to some hope for his 'powerful machine', but, after various disputes, some of his old supporters, including even the staunch Eccarius, deserted him. He was standing almost alone; what if the 'machine' should fall now into enemy hands?

The last full congress took place at the Hague in September 1872. It was also the most representative; even Marx was there. Amid much tension, a motion was carried to increase the powers of the General Council, in the face of Marx's proposal to abolish it altogether. Then, according to a reporter, 'there was a slight pause. It was the lull before the storm...Up got Engels, Marx's right hand, and said he would make a communication to the Congress.' Engels recommended that the seat of the General Council be moved to New York. 'Consternation and discomfiture stood plainly written on the faces of the party of dissension...It was some time before anyone rose to speak. It was a coup d'état...'

Despite the shock caused by this completely unexpected proposal, the motion was carried by a narrow majority, with many abstentions. Marx had achieved what he wanted: in order to save the International from his enemies he had effectively destroyed it. After struggling on for four more years it was formally dissolved in Philadelphia in 1876.

Whether it could ever have been the 'powerful machine' that Marx envisaged is a matter for debate. Individual membership (as opposed to affiliated membership of unions and similar organisations) was never large: in Britain by the end of 1870 the total of individual members was only 254. But, in the right hands, and with all the different national factions in harmony instead of at odds, it might have come to something. Who can say?

The Fire Goes Out

1872 – 1883

FROM THAT MOMENT at the Hague congress Marx began to lead a much quieter life. He became more even-tempered, and studiously avoided all public debate, though he still held his beliefs as fervently as ever. He settled into a daily routine: working in the morning, going for a walk after lunch, having dinner at six and entertaining friends at nine. The most frequent visitor now was Engels, who had moved to a fine house in Regent's Park, only a few minutes' walk away, in 1870. He and Marx often spent whole afternoons pacing up and down, wearing out the carpet in Marx's study, or strolling on Hampstead Heath.

In 1875 the Marxes moved for the last time, just along to a smaller, elegant house at 41 Maitland Park Road; and, with Engels in close attendance, there were at last no more financial worries.

By now the three daughters were establishing their own lives. On 2 April 1868 Laura had married Paul Lafargue at St Pancras Registry Office. Lafargue, a medical student and disciple of Proudhon who had come to London as a delegate to the General Council of the International, did not immediately inspire Marx's approval, especially as Laura had displayed little apparent affection for him. But after investigating Lafargue's background Marx came to like him well enough, and there was no danger of parental disapproval of the match. After the Hague congress the Lafargues settled in London, where, when Paul had failed in a venture to set up a photo-engraving firm, they lived comfortably on Engels's donations. They had three children, none of whom survived infancy.

In October 1872, at the same registry office, Jenny married Charles Longuet, a penniless refugee of the Commune. After a brief period in Oxford they too came back to London, where Jenny could be near her beloved father; she confessed to Kugelmann that 'though married, my heart is as chained as it ever was to the spot where my Papa is, and life elsewhere would not be life to me.' She became a governess, while Longuet got a post lecturing in French at King's College. After a son who died in infancy, they had five children. Marx was particularly attached to the eldest of these, Jean or 'Johnny', whom he called 'the apple of my eye', and who must have reminded him of his own lost son.

Also in 1872 Eleanor became involved with Hippolyte-Prosper-Olivier Lissagaray, a flamboyant French Basque twice her age. He had been active in the Commune but was too much of an individualist to follow any particular ideology. Marx disapproved of their relationship, which went on more or less covertly until 1880, when Lissagaray was able to return to Paris. Eleanor did not go with him. Instead, she threw herself into political activity, and tried to build a career as an actress. Marx, despite his love of the theatre, was not keen on this; but, after her father's death, she did eventually make a contribution to contemporary theatre in association with Edward Aveling, with whom she lived unhappily for many years.

Marx loved his daughters dearly, and at least two of the three returned his love with complete devotion, knowing him affectionately as 'the Moor', on account of his dark complexion. Jenny was probably his favourite; but he saw his own character most reflected in the headstrong Eleanor. As Eleanor was to recall, 'Father was talking of my eldest sister and of me, and said: "Jenny is most like me, but Tussy...is me".'

Although Marx spent the last dozen years of his

The Fire Goes Out

life in financial security he was bedevilled by other problems, of a kind which no amount of help from Engels could solve. His earlier way of life had left an indelible scar on his health. He was suffering from pressure on the brain and incurable insomnia when, in May 1873, he was persuaded to consult Engels's doctor, Gumpert, in Manchester. Gumpert told him to work no more than four hours a day. He obeyed, and felt slightly better, but by autumn the headaches had come back, so he consulted Gumpert again. This time the doctor diagnosed a swollen liver and advised Marx to go to Karlsbad, a fashionable spa in Bohemia. Marx went instead to Harrogate for three weeks, accompanied by Eleanor, herself ill as a result of what he took to be hysteria over Lissagaray. The cure proved ineffective, insomnia continued to plague him, and in the winter the boils returned. In April 1874 he spent three weeks in Ramsgate, then in July went to the Isle of Wight, but had to hurry home to care for Eleanor. Now, at last, he decided to take Gumpert's advice and try Karlsbad.

The trip was arranged for Marx and Eleanor by Kugelmann, who went with them to the Germania, one of the less expensive hotels, where they arrived in August. Marx described himself in the official list of visitors as 'Herr Charles Marx, private gentleman', which he hoped would 'avoid the suspicion that I am the notorious Karl Marx'. To avert trouble with the police he had applied for naturalisation as a British subject before he left London, but the application was rejected by the Home Office. He was kept under constant police surveillance in Karlsbad, where his conduct was impeccable.

The cure, which he took very seriously, involved a mechanical daily ritual. He would be up by 5.30 and visit six springs, taking a glass of water at each, at fifteen-minute intervals. Breakfast consisted of special medicinal bread, after which there was an hour's walk and mid-morning coffee. Then came a walk around the hills, followed by a return to the hotel to change and have a nap before lunch, preceded every other day by a bath. After lunch there was more walking, then a light meal and early bed, all entertainments ending at 9 p.m. Marx enjoyed this life immensely, especially the long walks, and was inseparable from Eleanor. The only disruption of his happiness came from Kugelmann, who annoyed him with his 'carping criticism with which he quite needlessly embitters his own life and that of his family'.

After a couple of months at Karlsbad, Marx and Eleanor left on 21 September. Visiting friends on the way, they arrived back in London in early October.

The next year he went to Karlsbad alone. The cure was so effective that in October 1875 Engels could write, 'Marx has come back from Karlsbad quite changed, strong, fresh, confident and healthy, and can now once more take up his work in earnest.'

In fact he worked very little. He no longer had the sustained passionate interest, let alone the strength. As new editions of *Capital* in other languages appeared, so he would be pressed for Volumes Two and Three, but he made only vague attempts to work them up and his heart was not in it. He could still study: he learnt Russian in order to read about the evolution of agriculture in Russia with a view to using it as background material in Volume Three, and made copious notes on the subject, but he could no longer synthesise, no longer create. There were occasional flashes of the old fire, as in 1875 when he wrote what became known as the *Critique of the Gotha Programme*, attacking the union of the two German proletarian parties, the Lassallean ADAV and the more recent Eisenach party, at Gotha in May. For the most part he was content to sit back and play the role of respectable retired gentleman.

In 1876 he went again to Karlsbad, this time with Eleanor, whom he had missed greatly the year before. In 1877, however, he chose the minor spa of Neuenahr in the Rhineland, justifying himself to Engels by claiming that Karlsbad would be too expensive, and a new régime might do him good. It had the opposite effect. From the moment he gave up Karlsbad his health was in decline. In 1878 he

The Fire Goes Out

had to make do with Malvern, Bismarck's anti-socialist laws preventing him from going to Germany or Austria. He was accompanied by his wife, daughter Jenny, and grandson Jean, who were all very ill.

In 1879 he went to Jersey. By now he was preoccupied not so much with his own illness as with his wife's, an incurable cancer of the liver. In 1880 he took her to see Gumpert in Manchester, then to stay in Ramsgate. Marx was mentally and physically exhausted by the pathetic quest for health; the subject of sickness dominated his letters, even more than poverty had in years gone by. The fire was dying. As a public figure, he was a spent force.

There had been some comfort for him in the company of his grandchildren, and when the Longuets left for France in February 1881 he was heartbroken to be separated from the children who were 'inexhaustible sources of life and joy'. For weeks after they had gone, he wrote to Jenny Longuet, 'I often run to the window when I hear the voices of children...unaware, for a moment, that they are the other side of the Channel.'

His wife's health had deteriorated rapidly; by June 1881 it was clear that she was dying. In October, Marx himself fell ill and had to stay in bed for two months with bronchitis. Eleanor sat with him for many nights, and for three agonising weeks he was unable to visit Jenny in the next room. Eleanor later wrote:

> It was a terrible time. Our dear mother lay in the big front room, Moor in the small room behind. And the two of them, who were so used to one another, so close to one another, could not even be together in the same room...Never shall I forget the morning when he felt strong enough to go into Mother's room. When they were together they were young again - she a young girl and he a loving youth, both on the threshold of life, not an old man devastated by illness and an old dying woman parting from each other for ever.

Mercifully, it was only in the last few days that

Jenny suffered excruciating pain, and it was eased by morphia. When she died on 2 December, Marx told his daughter Jenny it was 'a gentle going to sleep, her eyes fuller, more beautiful, lighter than ever.' Her last word was 'good'. So they parted: as much in love, having endured so many hopes, disappointments and hardships together, as they had been as teenagers, all those years ago in Trier.

He was shattered by her death. He was unable even to go to her funeral because of his illness and the dreadful weather. He could distract himself only by concentrating on his own suffering, finding that 'the only effective antidote for sorrows of the spirit is bodily pain'. Partially recovered from bronchitis, he felt doubly crippled, 'morally through the loss of my wife, and physically through a thickening of the pleura'. In January 1882 he went with Eleanor to Ventnor; but the company was moribund, she on the verge of a nervous breakdown, while his coughing and bronchial catarrh were as bad as ever.

Disillusioned with Eleanor, neglected by the selfish Laura and unheeded by Jenny, herself ill and busy with her babies, Marx took the advice of Engels and Gumpert and went alone to Algiers. He was for once glad to get away from Engels, who was too boisterous for his liking now; he wrote to Jenny: 'Good old Fred may easily kill someone out of love.' After two-and-a-half sad and lonely months in Algiers he left in May 1882 for a month in Monte Carlo.

There was no rest now from his pleurisy and bronchitis. On 6 June he left for Argenteuil, where he spent three months at the home of the Longuets, seeking solace in 'the noise of children, this "microscopic world" that is much more interesting than the "macroscopic".' But there was little solace to be found. Jenny was in poor health and expecting another baby in September; and she had no help from her indolent husband. In the summer, Lenchen came to look after Jenny, and it was not long before Eleanor and Laura also gravitated to Argenteuil. Laura agreed to accompany Marx on a trip to Vevey in Switzerland, from which they

The Fire Goes Out

returned after Jenny had given birth to her only daughter.

Marx decided he was too much of a burden to Jenny, and came back to London. In October he went alone to Ventnor, and, feeling a little better, spent hours wandering over the downs on the Isle of Wight.

Jenny Longuet's health was now in rapid decline. Since April she had suffered severe pains from what was probably cancer of the bladder. Ignored by her husband, she was 'sunk in a torpor broken by nightmares and fantastic dreams' by the beginning of 1883, when the Lafargues saw her, and she died on 11 January, aged 38. It fell to Eleanor to break the news to Marx. She wrote: 'I have lived many a sad hour, but none so bad as that. I felt that I was bringing my father his death sentence. I racked my brain all the long anxious way to find how I could break the news to him. But I did not need to, my face gave me away. Moor said at once "our Jennychen is dead".'

The death of his favourite daughter was the knell for Marx. The fire which had been flickering ominously since his wife died was about to be snuffed out. He could not speak, from laryngitis; but then, there was nothing more to say. At home in London, Lenchen tried in vain to rekindle his appetite with tasty meals. He had mustard baths to warm his feet, and drank a pint of milk a day and a bottle of brandy in four. Bronchitis was complicated by an ulcer in the lung. By the end of February he was confined shivering to his room.

On 10 March, Engels told Laura that the doctor thought Marx's health was improving, that all would be well if he could get through the next two months. The will to fight was gone, however. On the 14th Marx took wine, milk and soup in the morning; but when Engels came in the afternoon 'the house was in tears, it seemed the end had come. I asked for information, tried to get a realistic view of the situation and to offer comfort. There had been a small haemorrhage and a sudden deterioration had set in. Our good old Lenchen who cared for him as no mother ever did for her child, went up and then came down again: he was half-asleep, would I come with her? When we entered, he sat there sleeping, but never to wake any more. In two minutes he had quietly and painlessly passed away.'

Marx died, contemptuous of bourgeois society to the last, intestate and stateless. He was buried in a simple grave, where his wife already lay, in a far corner of Highgate Cemetery on 17 March 1883. Although he wanted no more than that, the grave was moved to a more prominent position in 1954, and in 1956 a huge granite plinth, surmounted by a bronze head of Marx, was erected. The plinth bears the legend: *'Workers of all lands, unite'*; while the base of the monument carries the eleventh thesis on Feuerbach: *'The philosophers have only interpreted the world in various ways; the point is, to change it.'*

It was Karl Marx's disciple V.I. Lenin who transformed the philosopher's theories into violent action, which he was certain that both Marx and Engels would have approved. Writing a eulogy of the latter, who had just died in London on 5 August 1895, aged 74, Lenin claimed:

> They both knew Russian and read Russian books, took a lively interest in the country, followed the revolutionary movement with sympathy and maintained contact with Russian revolutionaries. They both became socialists after being democrats, and the democratic feeling of hatred for political despotism was extremely strong in them... That is why the heroic struggle of the handful of Russian revolutionaries against the mighty tsarist government evoked a most sympathetic echo in the hearts of these tried revolutionaries.

In fact, a year after the publication of *Capital*, Marx had been amused to learn that its first translated edition had appeared in the only country where any notice had been taken of it, yet to which he had always believed his theories had no application - Russia. He wrote to Kugelmann:

The Fire Goes Out

> It is an irony of fate that the Russians, whom I have fought unceasingly for twenty-five years and not only in Germany but in France and England, too, have always been my 'patrons'... But one must not take it too seriously... They always snatch at the most extreme things the West offers.

He was the apostle of class-hatred, which he considered the most potent influence in all history and the means by which the capitalist society and its institutions could be overthrown. That there are other factors which motivate and divide men does not seem to have occurred to him, and he would have brusquely dismissed any suggestion that he might, perhaps, have left them unconsidered.

Perhaps the most poignant comment on Marx's life, with all its tragedies for him and those who loved him, was made by his mother: 'If only Karl had *made* Capital, instead of just *writing* about it.' By merely writing about it, though, he had changed the world.

Karl Marx

1818 – 1883

The house in Trier where Karl Marx was born, 5 May 1818.

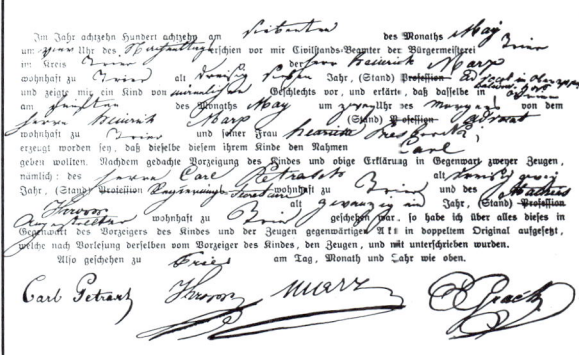

Marx's birth certificate.

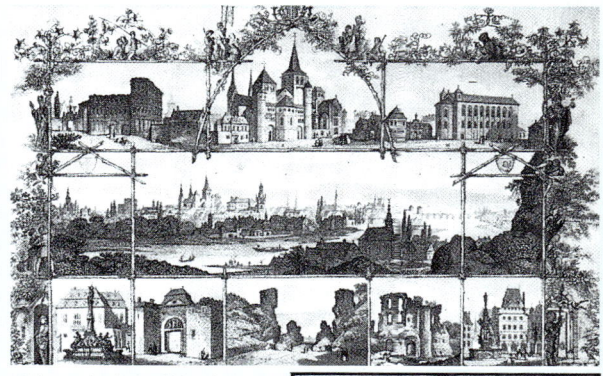

Trier at the time of Marx's childhood.

The young student in Bonn, Marx in 1836 aged eighteen, the earliest known likeness.

Jenny von Westphalen (1814-1881) about the time of their meeting. Four years older than Karl, they were married on 19 June 1843.

Trier student club in Bonn. Marx is shown in the back row marked with an 'X'. (The previous picture of Marx aged eighteen is an enlargement from this sketch).

A contemporary print of Humboldt University in Berlin, 'a workhouse by comparison with the Bacchanalian character of other Universities.' Marx studied here for 4½ years from October 1836 to March 1841.

G.W.F. Hegel (1770-1831). Among the major German philosophers of the early 19th century.

Hegel lecturing at Berlin University in 1828.

Cologne in 1840, where Marx began his serious journalism. In 1842 he became editor of the *Rhenish Gazette (Rheinische Zeitung)* and met Friedrich Engels for the first time.

The *Rhenish Gazette (Rheinische Zeitung)*. This progressive journal was first published on 1 January 1842 but was finally suppressed on 1 April 1843.

Moses Hess (1812-1875). Influential German Socialist who worked with Marx on the *Rhenish Gazette*.

Marx as Prometheus, a contemporary allegory on the suppression of the *Rhenish Gazette* in April 1843.

Paris in the mid-nineteenth century. An engraving by Edmund Evans. Karl and Jenny arrived in 1843 and their first daughter, also named Jenny, was born here on 1 May 1844.
Inset: Friedrich Engels (1820-1895), a photograph taken in 1845.

Brussels at the time of Marx's arrival after expulsion from France on 25 January 1845.

Edgar Marx (1846-1855). Karl and Jenny's first son, nicknamed 'Musch' or 'little fly', a frail child whose tragic life would epitomise the sorrows that were soon to engulf the family.

Helene Demuth (1820-1890), the faithful maid 'Lenchen', who kept house for the family until Marx's death and who had a son (Freddy) by Karl in June 1851.

Pierre-Joseph Proudhon (1809-1865), the eminent French Socialist.

A procession attending the Chartist petition to the House of Commons in 1842.

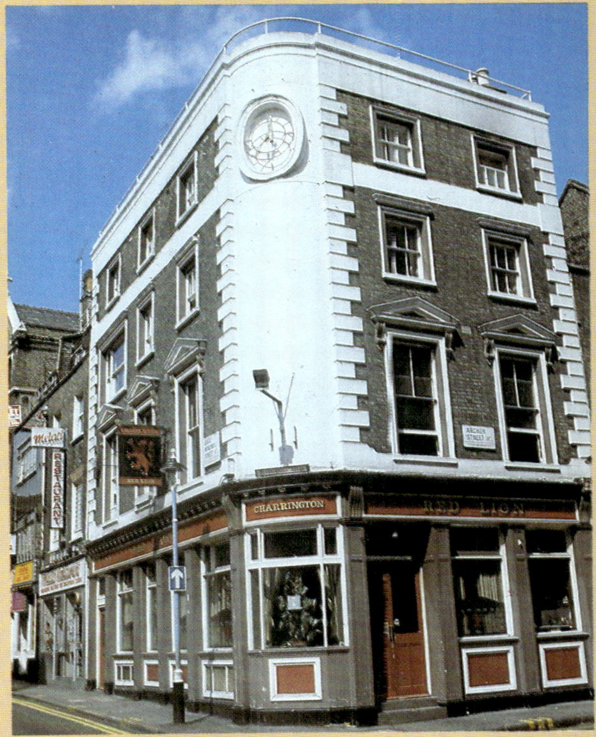

The Red Lion. A Soho public house where the German Workers Education Society, founded in 1840, met upstairs.

Title-page of the *Communist Manifesto*. The first German edition was published in February 1848.

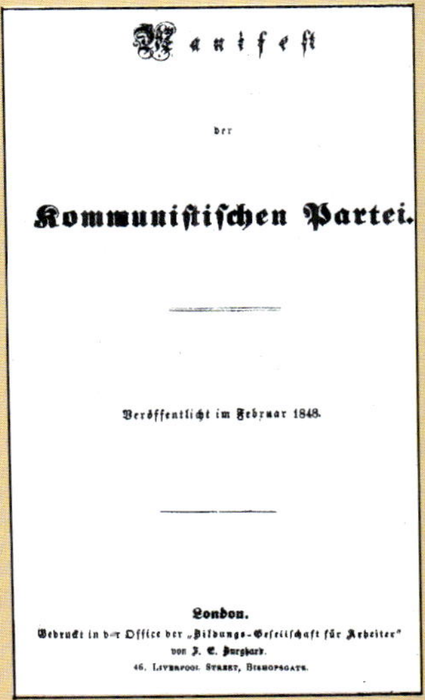

Manifest

der

Kommunistischen Partei.

Veröffentlicht im Februar 1848.

London.

Gedruckt in der Office der „Bildungs-Gesellschaft für Arbeiter"

von J. E. Burghard.

46, Liverpool Street, Bishopsgate.

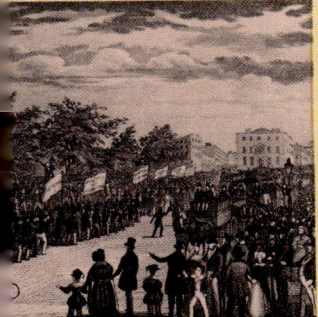

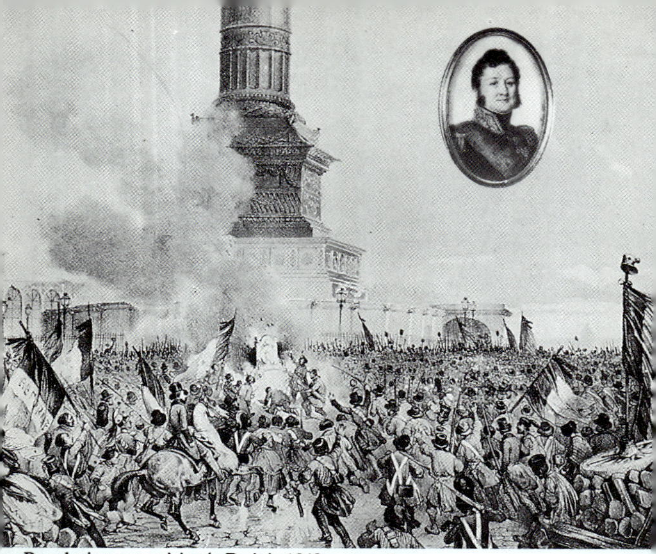

Revolutionary uprising in Paris in 1848. The mob burning the Emperor's throne in the Place Vendôme.

Inset: Louis Philippe (1773-1850).

The *New Rhenish Gazette (Neue Rheinische Zeitung)*. First published 1 June 1848, it ran for 301 issues until 18 May 1849.

Neue Rheinische Zeitung.

Organ der Demokratie.

29. Köln, Donnerstag 29. Juni

Französische Republik.

Westphalen.

Marx and Engels proof-reading a copy of the *New Rhenish Gazette*.

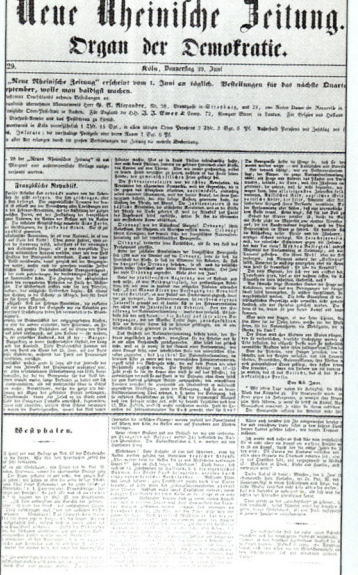

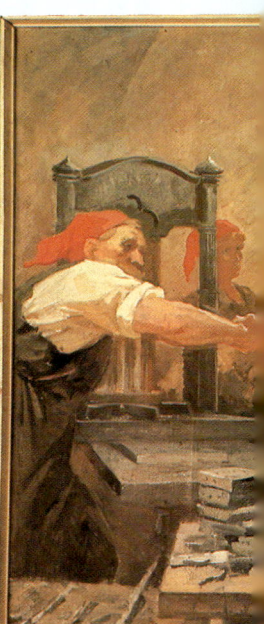

Marx's passport dated at Paris, 24 August 1849, the date he sailed for England.

(P. G.)

POLICE GÉNÉRALE DE FRANCE

Passe-Port

gratuit

valable pour un an.

DÉPARTEMENT de la Seine

SOUS-PRÉFECTURE de Police

COMMUNE de Paris

Registre des Etrang. N° 800

SIGNALEMENT

Age de 32 ans

taille d'un mètre 75 centimètres.

cheveux noirs

front haut

sourcils bruns

yeux bruns

nez ordinaire

bouche moyenne

barbe noire

menton rond

visage rond

teint ordinaire

SIGNES PARTICULIERS

Signature du Porteur: Dr. Ch. Marx

RÉPUBLIQUE FRANÇAISE.

Liberté, Égalité, Fraternité

Passe-port Gratuit,

valable pour un an.

Nous Préfet de Police

Invitons les Autorités civiles et militaires à laisser passer et librement circuler de Paris département de la Seine en Angleterre département

M. Marx, Charles

profession de Docteur en philosophie

natif de Trèves, Prusse département de Rhénanie

demeurant à Paris, rue de Lille 45

et à lui donner aide et protection, en cas de besoin.

Délivré sur note

Fait à Paris, le 24 août 1849

Le Préfet de Police

Le Chef de bureau

Le Secrétaire Gal

PRÉFECTURE DE POLICE

Gratis.

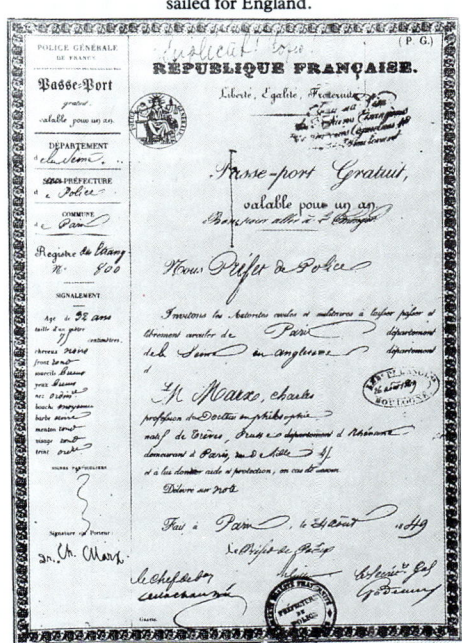

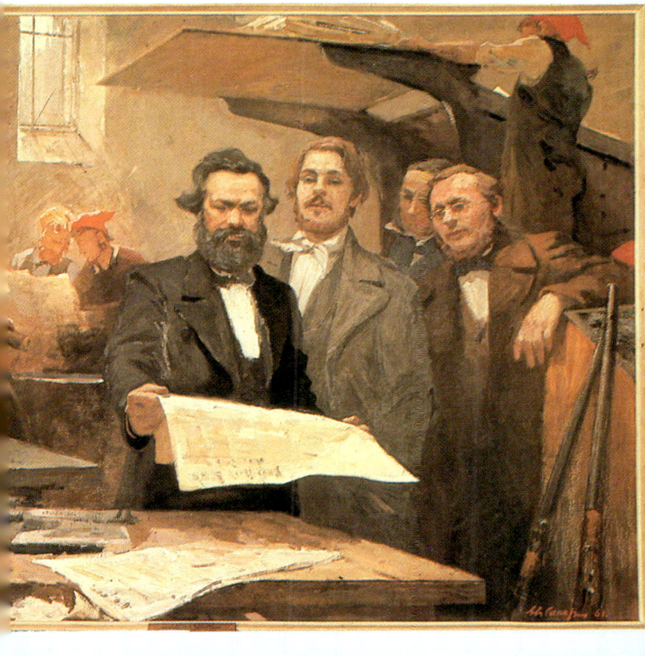

4 Anderson Street, Chelsea. The first family home in London until evicted in March 1850.

The Chartist Convention in London, 1848.

The former German Hotel off Leicester Square, where the Marx family moved after eviction from Anderson Street.

Manchester in the mid-nineteenth century.

28 Dean Street, Soho, today. The Marx family lived in two rooms on the top floor until 1856. Their time here was one of dreadful poverty and squalor and three of their children died here.

The British Museum in Bloomsbury.

The Reading Room of the British Museum.

Karl Marx's favourite seat in the Reading Room, number O7.

Title-page of *The Eighteenth Brumaire of Louis Napoleon* published in 1852.

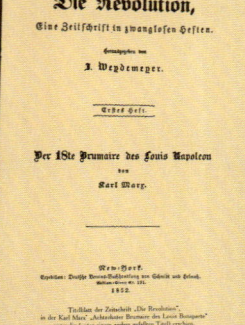

46 Grafton Terrace (formerly 9), Kentish Town. Two small inheritances enabled the family to move from Dean Street in 1856. They remained here until 1864.

Jenny Marx with their oldest daughter Jenny, around 1854.

Holiday time on Hampstead Heath, a contemporary print.

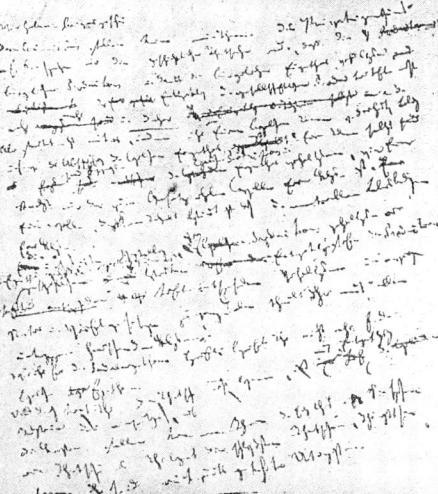

An example of Marx's terrible handwriting.

A plague spot near the London gasworks, South Lambeth, in the mid-nineteenth century.

The appalling condition of the poor, 'A Court for King Cholera', a cartoon by Leech from *Punch* in 1852.

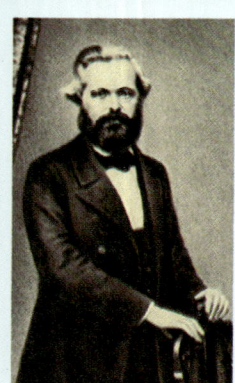

Karl Marx in 1861.

St Martin's Hall, off Covent Garden, now demolished, where at a meeting on 25 September 1864 it was proposed that the International Working Men's Association be formed.

INTERN^L WORKING MEN'S ASSOC^N № 5431 ASSOCIATION INTERN^LE DES OUVRIERS

INTERN^LE ARBEITER ASSOC^N ASSOC^NE INTERN^LE D'OPERAI.

MEMBER'S ANNUAL SUBSCRIPTION CARD.

Frederick Engels was admitted a Member on the First day of January 1865 and paid as his Annual Subscription £

Geo Odger — President of Central Council.

G. W. Wheeler. — Honorary Treasurer.

E. Dupont — Corresponding Secretary for France.

Karl Marx — Germany.

— Italy.

Emile Holtorp — Poland.

H. Jung. — Switzerland.

W R Cremer — Honorary General Secretary.

INTERNATIONAL WORKING ASSOCIATION CENTRAL COUNCIL LONDON

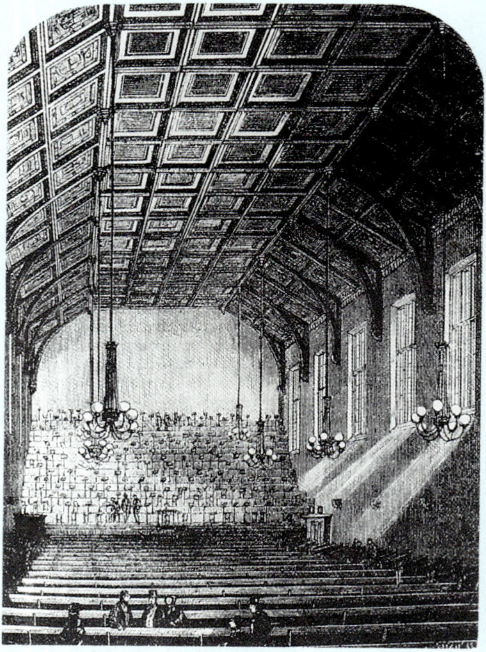

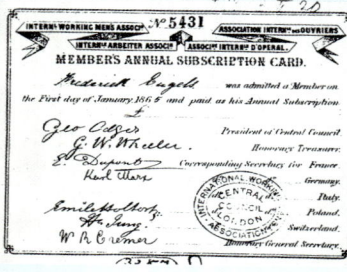

Engels's membership card to IWMA with Marx's signature as Council Secretary for Germany.

Engels with Marx and his daughters, Jenny, Laura and Eleanor in 1864.

Charles Longuet (1839-1903).

Jenny (1844-1883).

Eleanor (1855-1898).

Edward Aveling (1851-1898).

Paul Lafargue (1842-1911).

Laura (1845-1911).

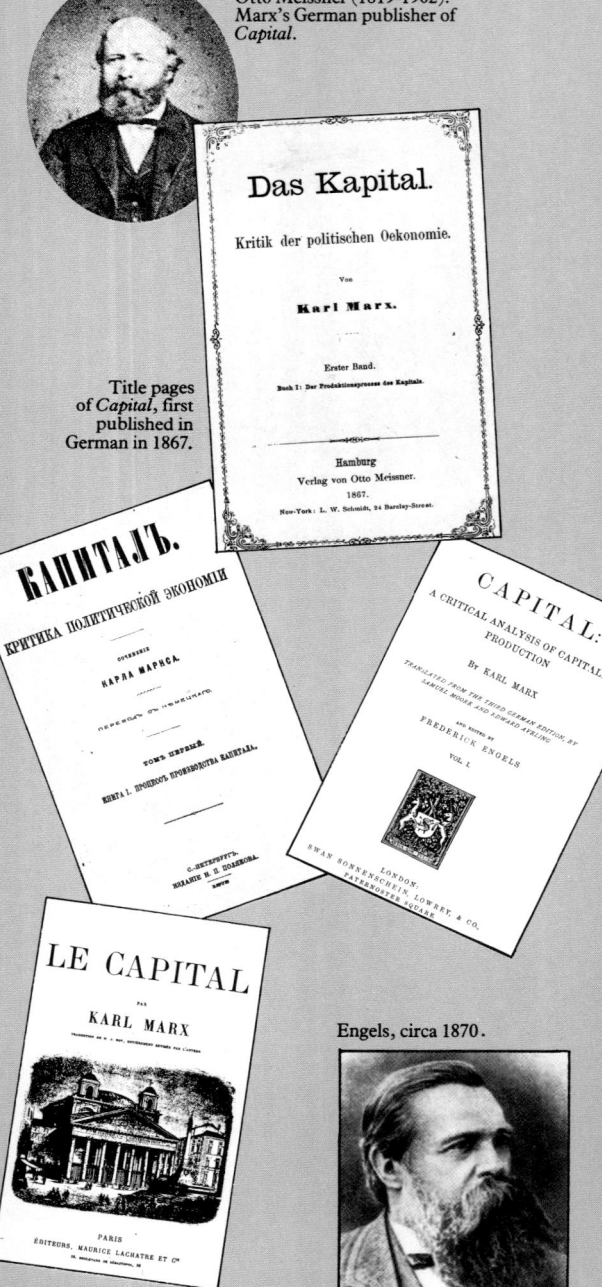

Otto Meissner (1819-1902). Marx's German publisher of *Capital*.

Title pages of *Capital*, first published in German in 1867.

Engels, circa 1870.

Marx in 1867, the year *Capital* was first published.

International Working Men's Association Congress in Geneva, 1866.

IWMA Congress in Basle, 1869.

The London Stock Exchange, a contemporary print.

Regent Street, a mid-nineteenth century view of 'fashionable' London.

Proclamation of the Paris Commune on 28 March 1871. Tens of thousands of Communards were slaughtered by government troops before the rebellion was crushed at the end of May.

Street barricades in Paris

The ruins in Paris after the rebellion.

Mikhail Bakunin (1814-1876). Europe's leading anarchist and colleague of Marx and Engels.

Poster advertising a meeting on the first anniversary of the Paris Commune, with Marx as one of the speakers.

1 Modena Villas, Maitland Park Road, where Marx lived from 1864 until his death in 1883.

Marx in 1872.

122 Regent's Park Road. Engels's home from 1870 to 1894.

Engels in 1893.

The house in Ventnor, Isle of Wight, where Marx convalesced during the winter of 1882-83.

Karl Marx (1818-1883).

Early Trade Union banners.

George Julian Harney (1817-1897).

Bruno Bauer (1809-1882).

Ludwig Feuerbach (1804-1872).

Wilhelm Wolff (1809-1864).

George Odger (1820-1877).

WilLam Liebknecht (1826-1900).

Louis Kugelmann (1828-1902).

Ferdinand Lassalle (1825-1864).

Jenny Marx shortly before her death on 2 December 1881.

Karl Marx's signature.

Family Tree.

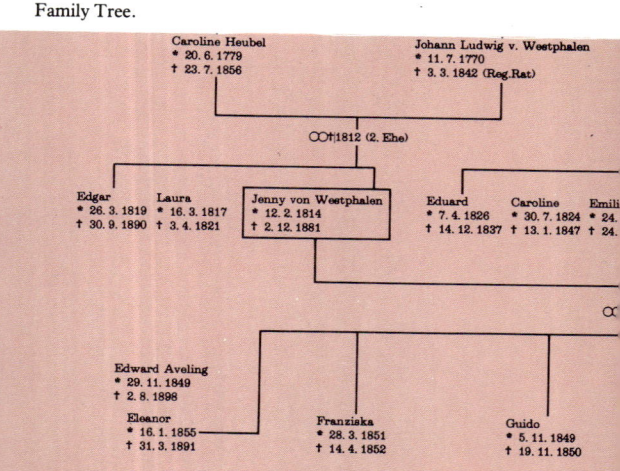

Karl Marx in 1875.

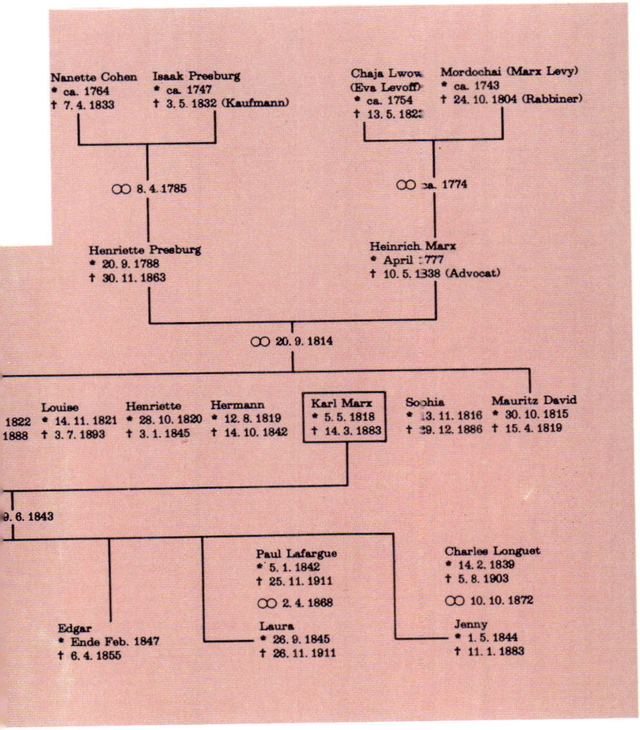

The much-visited Karl Marx memorial and grave, Highgate Cemetery, North London.

Not all visitors come to pay respects.

Highgate Cemetery.

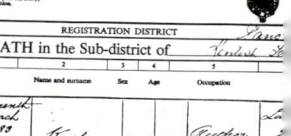

Karl Marx's death certificate, showing 'Laryngitis 2 months' as the cause on 14 March 1883.

A tablet marks the original grave. In 1954 the grave was moved to a more prominent position and a bronze head commissioned by the Communist Party of Great Britain was unveiled in 1956.

Marx in Algiers, taking a cure in 1882 the last known photograph.

ACKNOWLEDGEMENTS

The author and publishers would like to thank the following for their kind permission in supplying the quotations and illustrations in this book.

Quotations:

Estate of G. Bernard Shaw, Society of Authors, London

Illustrations:

BBC Hulton Picture Library, London
British Library, London
British Museum, London
Friedrich Ebert Stiftung, Trier
Gruppo Editoriale Fabbri, Milan
Institut für Marxismus-Leninismus, Berlin
International Institute for Social History, Amsterdam
Mansell Collection, London
Marx Memorial Library, London
Museum of London
National Museum of Labour History, London
Snark International, Paris
SPD Archiv, Berlin
Evergreen Lives Archive
Evergreen Lives Archive/Photo: Lennox Smillie